Grammar Dimensions

Book 2B
Form, Meaning, and Use

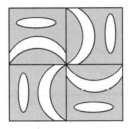

Heidi Riggenbach

University of Washington

Virginia Samuda

Sonoma State University

Heinle & Heinle Publishers
A Division of Wadsworth, Inc.
Boston, Massachusetts 02116 U.S.A

Edyta Sawoświat

Photo Credits:

Photos on page 2 (photos 1–3) courtesy of H. Armstrong Roberts.

Photo on page 2 (photo 4) by J. Myers courtesy of H. Armstrong Roberts.

Photos on page 2 (photos 5, 6) courtesy of the University of Illinois.

Photo on page 2 (photo 7) courtesy of the *Illio,* University of Illinois yearbook.

Photo on page 38 of John Lennon courtesy of Kahana/Shooting Star.

Photo on page 177 of Diana Ross (recent) courtesy of Kahana/Shooting Star, page 178 (yearbook) courtesy of Seth Poppel Yearbook Archives.

Photo on page 177 of Tina Turner (recent) courtesy of McAfee/Shooting Star, page 178 (yearbook) courtesy of Seth Poppel Yearbook Archives.

Photo on page 177 of Madonna (recent) courtesy of Archer/Shooting Star, page 178 (yearbook) courtesy of Seth Poppel Yearbook Archives.

Photo on page 177 of Meryl Streep (recent) courtesy of Leonelli/Shooting Star, page 178 (yearbook) courtesy of Seth Poppel Yearbook Archives.

Photo on page 177 of Bruce Springsteen (recent) courtesy of Gallo/Shooting Star, page 178 (yearbook) courtesy of Seth Poppel Yearbook Archives.

Photo on page 177 of Warren Beatty (recent) courtesy of Fotex/Shooting Star, page 178 (yearbook) courtesy of Seth Poppel Yearbook Archives.

The publication of the Grammar Dimensions series
was directed by the members of the Heinle & Heinle
ESL Publishing Team:

David C. Lee, Editorial Director
Susan Mraz, Marketing Manager
Lisa McLaughlin, Production Editor
Nancy Mann, Developmental Editor

Also participating in the publication of this program were:

Publisher: Stanley J. Galek
Editorial Production Manager: Elizabeth Holthaus
Assistant Editor: Kenneth Mattsson
Manufacturing Coordinator: Mary Beth Lynch
Full Service Production/Design: Publication Services, Inc.
Cover Designer: Martucci Studio
Cover Artist: Susan Johnson

10   9   8   7   6   5   4   3   2   1

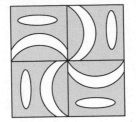

Book 2B Table of Contents

(See page vii for Book 2A Table of Contents)

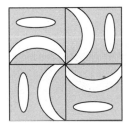

Book 2A Table of Contents

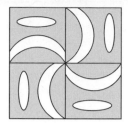

Preface to *Grammar Dimensions: Form, Meaning, and Use*

To the Teacher

ABOUT THE SERIES

With the recent emphasis on communication, the teaching of grammar has often been downplayed, or even overlooked entirely. Although one would not want to argue the goal of having students be able to communicate successfully, it is important to recognize that a major means to this end is to teach students to use grammatical structures. Some grammatical structures may be acquired naturally without instruction, but it is assumed by the creators of this series that explicit focus on the troublesome aspects of English will facilitate and accelerate their acquisition. The teaching needs to be done, however, in such a way that the interdependence of grammar and communication is appreciated.

In this regard, it is crucial to recognize that the use of grammatical structures involves more than having students achieve formal accuracy. Students must be able to use the structures meaningfully and appropriately as well. This series, therefore, takes into account all three dimensions of language: syntax/morphology (form), semantics (meaning), and pragmatics (use). The relevant facts about the **form, meaning,** and **use** of English grammatical structures were compiled into a comprehensive scope and sequence and distributed across a four-book series. Where the grammatical system is complex (e.g., the verb-tense system) or the structure complicated (e.g., the passive voice), it is revisited in each book in the series. Nevertheless, each book is free-standing and may be used independently of the others in the series if the student or program needs warrant.

Another way in which the interdependence of grammar and communication is stressed is that students first encounter every structure in a meaningful context where their attention is not immediately drawn to its formal properties. Each treatment of a grammatical structure concludes with students being given the opportunity to use the structure in communicative activities. The point of the series is not to teach grammar as static knowledge, but to have students use it in the dynamic process of communication. In this way grammar might better be thought of as a skill, rather than as an area of knowledge.

It is my hope that this book will provide teachers with the means to create, along with their students, learning opportunities that are tailored to learners' needs, are enjoyable, and will maximize everyone's learning.

ABOUT THE BOOK

This book deals with basic sentence and subsentence grammatical structures. It also introduces language forms that support certain social functions such as making requests and seeking permission.

Units that share certain features have been clustered together. No more than three or four units are clustered at one time, however, in order to provide for some variety of focus. As the units have been designed to stand independently, it is possible for a syllabus to be constructed that follows a different order of structures than the one presented in the book. It is also not expected that there will be sufficient time to deal with all the material that has been introduced here within a single course. Teachers are encouraged to see the book as a resource from which they can select units or parts of units which best meet student needs.

Unit Organization

TASKS

One way in which to identify student needs is to use the **Tasks**, which open each unit as a pre-test. Learner engagement in the Tasks may show that students have already learned what they need to know about a certain structure, in which case the unit can be skipped entirely. Or it may be possible, from examining students' performance, to pinpoint precisely where the students need to work. For any given structure, the learning challenge presented by the three dimensions of language is not equal. Some structures present more of a form-based challenge to learners; for others, the long-term challenge is to learn what the structures mean or when to use them. The type and degree of challenge varies according to the inherent complexity of the structure itself and the particular language background and level of English proficiency of the students.

FOCUS BOXES

Relevant facts about the form, meaning, and use of the structure are presented in **Focus Boxes** following the Task. Teachers can work their way systematically through a given unit or can pick and choose from among the Focus Boxes those points on which they feel students specifically need to concentrate.

EXERCISES

From a pedagogical perspective, it is helpful to think of grammar as a skill to be developed. Thus, in this book, **Exercises** have been provided to accompany each Focus Box. Certain of the Exercises may be done individually, others with students working in pairs or in small groups. Some of the Exercises can be done in class, others assigned as homework. Students' learning styles and the learning challenge they are working on will help teachers determine the most effective way to have students use the Exercises. (The Instructor's Manual should be consulted also for helpful hints in this regard.)

ACTIVITIES

At the end of each unit are a series of **Activities** that help students realize the communicative value of the grammar they are learning and that offer them further practice in using the grammar to convey meaning. Teachers or students may select the Activities from which they believe they would derive the most benefit and enjoyment. Student performance on these Activities can be used as a post-test as well. Teachers should not expect perfect performance at this point, however. Often there is a delayed effect in learning anything, and even some temporary backsliding in student performance as new material is introduced.

OTHER COMPONENTS

An **Instructor's Manual** is available for this book. The Manual contains answers to the Exercise questions and grammatical notes where pertinent. The Manual also further discusses the theory underlying the series and "walks a teacher through" a typical unit, suggesting ways in which the various components of the unit might be used and supplemented in the classroom.

A student **Workbook** also accompanies this book. It provides additional exercises to support the material presented in this text. Many of the workbook exercises are specially designed to help students prepare for the TOEFL (Test of English as a Foreign Language).

Each level of Grammar Dimensions is available in split editions (A and B) or as a complete text. The split editions are ideal for short course or classes which move at a gradual pace.

To the Student

All grammar structures have a form, a meaning, and a use. We can show this with a pie chart:

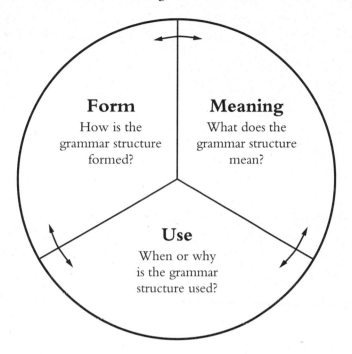

Often you will find that you know the answer to one or more of these questions, but not to all of them, for a particular grammar structure. This book has been written to help you learn answers to these questions for the major grammar structures of English. More importantly, it gives you practice with the answers so that you can develop your ability to use English grammar structures accurately, meaningfully, and appropriately.

At the beginning of each unit, you will be asked to work on a **Task.** The Task will introduce you to the grammar structures to be studied in the unit. However, it is not important at this point that you think about grammar. You should just do the Task as well as you can.

In the next section of the unit are **Focus Boxes** and **Exercises.** You will see that the boxes are labeled with **FORM, MEANING, USE,** or a combination of these, corresponding to the three parts of the pie chart. In each Focus Box is information that answers one or more of the questions in the pie. Along with the Focus Box are Exercises that should help you put into practice what you have studied.

The last section of each unit contains communicative **Activities.** Hopefully, you will enjoy doing these and at the same time receive further practice using the grammar structures in meaningful ways.

By working on the Task, studying the Focus Boxes, doing the Exercises, and engaging in the Activities, you will develop greater knowledge of English grammar and skill in using it. I also believe you will enjoy the learning experience along the way.

Diane Larsen-Freeman

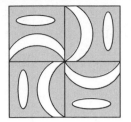

Acknowledgments

Series Director Acknowledgments

As with any project this ambitious, a number of people have made important contributions. I need to thank my students in the MAT Program at the School for International Training and audiences worldwide for listening to me talk about my ideas for reconciling the teaching of grammar with communicative language teaching. Their feedback and questions have been invaluable in the evolution of my thinking. One student, Anna Mussman, should be singled out for her helpful comments on the manuscript that she was able to provide based on her years of English teaching. A number of other anonymous teacher reviewers have also had a formative role in the development of the series. I hope they derive some satisfaction in seeing that their concerns were addressed wherever possible. In addition, Marianne Celce-Murcia not only helped with the original scope and sequence of the series, but also provided valuable guidance throughout its evolution.

I feel extremely grateful, as well, for the professionalism of the authors, who had to put into practice the ideas behind this series. Their commitment to the project, patience with its organic nature, and willingness to keep at it are all much appreciated. I insisted that the authors be practicing ESL teachers. I believe the series has benefited from this decision, but I am also cognizant of the demands it has put on the authors' lives these past few years.

Finally, I must acknowledge the support of the Heinle and Heinle "team." This project was "inherited" by Heinle and Heinle during its formative stage. To Dave Lee, Susan Mraz, Lisa McLaughlin, and especially Susan Maguire, who never stopped believing in this project, I am indeed thankful. And to Nancy Mann, who helped the belief become a reality, I am very grateful.

Author Acknowledgments

We would like to thank our families, friends, students, colleagues, cats—and each other—for hanging in there. We would also like to thank Diane Larsen-Freeman for her guidance during the process of writing this book, and the following reviewers for their valuable suggestions: Brian Hickey (Manhattanville College), Marilyn Santos (Valencia Community College), Marjore Walsleben (UCLA), Martha Low (University of Oregon), Jonathan Seeley (University of Arizona), and the field tester, Mary Monogue (University of Colorado, Boulder).

15

Requests and Permission

*Can/Could,
Will/Would, May*

Task

You are about to start house-sitting for a friend of yours. Your friend has left you a note with instructions about what to do while she is gone. Unfortunately, someone has spilled coffee on the note, and now it is difficult to read. Try to find the missing parts of the note from the choices on the next page. Write the appropriate number in the spaces on the note.

I'm glad you'll be here to watch the house while I'm gone! My neighbors think that this neighborhood is not completely safe at night, so (A)

The cats eat twice a day, (B)
I don't want them to stay out at night so (C)

The plants need to be watered twice a week. (D)

I left some bills to mail on the kitchen table. (E)

My cousin from out of town said that he would call this week. (F)

The rent check is on the kitchen table. It's due at the end of the week. (G)

I told the landlord about the broken light in the bathroom. If he calls, (H)

Thanks for everything. (I)

1. . . . could you ask him to fix it as soon as possible?
2. . . . remember to lock the windows and doors when it gets dark. Thanks.
3. . . . so will you please give them water on Tuesday and Friday?
4. . . . See you next week!
5. . . . Would you mind mailing them for me tomorrow morning?
6. . . . please make sure they come in around 8:00.
7. . . . Would you take a message and tell him I'll be back on the 29th?
8. . . . so could you feed them in the morning and at night?
9. . . . Please mail it before Friday.

Focus 1

FORM ● USE

Making Polite Requests

FORM
USE

- Questions using the modals *can, could, will,* and *would* are ways of making polite requests. If you really want someone to say yes to a request, it is important to make the request polite.
  - The modals *could* and *would* sound more polite than the modals *can* and *will.*
  - Providing some good background or reason for why you are making the request and using *please* are also ways to make requests sound more polite. In questions, *please* **usually** comes between the subject *you* and the verb.

    (a) I left my notes at home. Could you **please** lend me yours?
  - The reason for making the request can also come **after** the question.

    (b) Could you please lend me your notes? I left mine at home.
  - Another way to make a polite request is to use the phrase *Would you mind* + verb + *-ing.*

    (c) Would you mind lending me your notes?

Exercise 1

Below are some situations in which requests are commonly made. For each situation, make a polite request.

1. You want to know what time it is. You find someone who is wearing a watch and you say: ____

   _____ ?

2. When you pay for your groceries at the supermarket, you remember that you need some change. You hand the cashier a dollar and say: _____

   _____ ?

3. You have been waiting in line at the bank for 15 minutes, but you need to get a drink of water. You turn to the friendly-looking person standing behind you in line, and you say: _____

   _____ ?

4. You are watching a videotape in class. Your classmate in front of you is in the way. You want him or her to move his or her chair. You say: _____

   _____ ?

5. Your teacher just showed the class a videotape. It is finished; your classroom is dark. Your instructor wants the student who is sitting near the light switch to turn on the lights, so she or he says: _____

   _____ ?

6. There is a lot of noise outside your classroom. Your teacher wants the student who is sitting near the door to close it, so she or he says: _____

   _____ ?

7. A classmate is giving a presentation, but she is speaking very quietly. You cannot hear her. You say: _____ ?

Focus 2

Making Polite Refusals

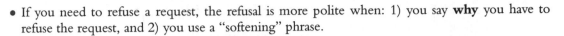

USE

- If you need to refuse a request, the refusal is more polite when: 1) you say **why** you have to refuse the request, and 2) you use a "softening" phrase.

Request	**"Softening" Phrase + Reason**
Can you lend me your notes?	**(a)** **I'm sorry**, but I need them to study for the test.
	(b) OR **I'm afraid** I didn't take any notes!
	(c) OR **I'd like to,** but I left mine at home too.

Exercise 2

Make requests of all your classmates and find someone who will grant your request (say yes) for the following things. For each request, try to find at least one person who will say yes. If a classmate says no, write down what the reason is for refusing your request (if a reason is given).

Request	Reason for Saying No
1. lend you some money	
2. buy you a cup of coffee	
3. tell you the name of a good bookstore	
4. give you a ride home after class	
5. teach you how to dance	

Focus 3

Responding to Requests

FORM

- To respond informally to requests, short answers are acceptable.

Request	Verbal Response
Can you lend me your notes?	**(a)** Sure.
	(b) You bet.
	(c) Yeah, no problem.
	(d) I'd be glad to.

- *Could* and *would* are usually not used in response to requests.

Can/Could you lend me your notes? **(e)** Yes, I can
NOT: Yes, I could.

Will/Would you lend me your notes? **(f)** Yes, I will
NOT: Yes, I would.

Exercise 3

Make polite requests for the following situations. Use *can, could, will, would,* or *would you mind* in these requests.

What is the response? How is the request politely accepted or refused?

1. You have a toothache. Your dentist asks you to sit back in the chair, open your mouth, and

point to the tooth that hurts. The dentist says: _____

_____ ?

What do you do or say? _____

_____ .

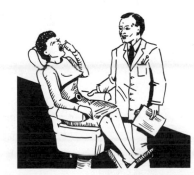

2. Your friend is helping you hang a picture on your wall. He is holding it up while you decide where it should go. You say: _____

_____ ?

What does your friend do or say? _____

_____ .

3. At your first exercise class, the instructor asks you to use the wall to get your spine in a straight position. The instructor says: _____

_____ ?

What do you do or say? _____

_____ .

4. There's a place on your back that suddenly begins to itch. You ask your close friend to scratch

it. You say: _____ ?

What does your friend do or say? _____

_____ .

But your friend is not quite getting the right place. So you say:_____

_____ ?

5. You are at a restaurant, and the people at the next table are smoking. You want them to stop, so

you say:_____

_____ ?

What do they do or say? _____

_____ .

Exercise 4

Place the following questions in the chart below, writing the number of each sentence in the appropriate box. The first one has been done for you.

Something the Speaker Wants to Do (request for permission)	Something the Speaker Wants Somebody Else to Do (general request)
1	

1. Could I smoke?
2. Can you open the window?
3. May I ask a question?
4. Could you speak more slowly?
5. Would you mind lending me your dictionary?
6. Can I leave early?
7. Would you tell me the answer?
8. May we swim in your pool?
9. Could you show us how to do it?
10. Could I borrow your knife?
11. Would you mind if I handed in my assignment a day late?

Focus 4

FORM ● USE

Asking for Permission

FORM
USE

- When you want **somebody** to do something, you can make a request. When **you** want to do something, and you want to find out if it is permitted or allowed, you can request permission:

  (a) Could I leave early? ⎫
  (b) Can I smoke in here? ⎬ Is it all right if I do this?
  (c) May I ask a question? ⎭

- In formal situations, *may* or *could* are used in questions to request permission. If the speaker thinks that the listener has a lot of authority or power, she or he uses *may* or *could*.

- As with requests, *can* is used in informal situations to ask for permission. If the speaker and the listener know each other well and / or have an equal amount of power, *can* is used.

  You can also politely ask for permission using *Would you mind* + *if* +**simple past tense.**

  (d) Would you mind if I asked you a question?

Exercise 5

For each answer, what was probably the question?

1. Question: _____?

   Teacher to student: No, I'd like you to hand it in on Friday. I announced the due date two weeks ago, so I'm afraid I won't be able to make any exceptions.

2. Question: _____?

   Friend to friend: Sure, it is a little cold in here.

3. Question: _____?

   Lecturer to member of the audience: Sorry, but I'm going to have to ask you to hold your questions until the end of my talk. We'll have 15 minutes for questions.

4. Question: _____?

   Secretary (on phone): Yes, may I tell him who's calling?

5. Question: _____?

12-year-old kid (on phone): Yeah, just a moment. I'll get him.

6. Question: _____?

Mother (to child): OK, you can have one more. But only **one**, because we're going to eat soon and I don't want you to spoil your appetite.

7. Question: _____?

Hostess to guest: Oh, of course, please help yourself. I'm glad you like them.

8. Question: _____?

Customer to salesperson: Yes, I want to look at the sweaters that are on sale. The ones that were advertised in the newspaper?

Focus 5

FORM ● USE

Responding to Requests for Permission

FORM
USE

- As with responses to requests, you can verbally answer requests for permission with short, positive phrases:

    Sure.   OK.   Yeah.   Of course.   No problem.

- If you need to refuse a request for permission, the refusal is more polite when you say **why** you have to refuse the request, and you use a "softening" phrase such as *Sorry*.

Exercise 6

For each of the following situations, work with another classmate to make general requests and requests for permission, and then respond to these requests. Decide how polite you need to be in each situation and whether *can, could, will, would, may,* or *would you mind* is the most appropriate to use. There is more than one way to ask and answer each question.

1. You are at a friend's house, and you want to use the phone.
2. Your teacher says something, but you do not understand, and you want her to repeat it.

3. Your friend has asked you to pick her up at the airport. You want to know if her flight, #255 from Denver, is on time, so you call the airline.

4. You want to borrow your roommate's car.

5. Your roommate is going to the store, and you remember that you need some film.

6. You are the first one to finish the reading test in class. You want to find out from your teacher if you are allowed to leave the room now.

7. It is very cold in class, and the window is open.

8. You see that your teacher is in her office with the door partly open. You want to go in to talk to her.

9. You are on the phone with the dentist's secretary because you want to change your appointment time.

10. You are at a close friend's house, and you would like a cup of tea.

11. Your friends have arrived at your house for dinner, and you want them to sit down.

12. You want to hold your friend's baby.

Activities

Activity 1

Go to a restaurant or cafeteria and pay attention to the different kinds of requests that are used. Try to observe five different requests. Take notes on these, using the chart below.

Observation Sheet		
Place:		
Time:		
Day:		
Request	**Who Made It**	**Response**

Discuss the results of your observations with other classmates. Were their observations similar? What words were used most often in requests: *can, could, will, would,* or *would you mind*?

Activity 2

Play this game in a group of five or six students or with the whole class. You are sick and cannot go out of your house. Choose a classmate and ask him or her to buy you something at the mall when she or he goes. Pick a letter from the alphabet. Your friend must think of something to buy that begins with the letter you choose, and then she or he must tell you what she or he will buy. She or he then chooses the next student and so on.

> **EXAMPLE: Shelley:** Bruno, would you please buy me something that begins with the letter *S*?
>
> **Bruno:** Sure. I'll buy you some stamps. Sue, could you buy me something that begins with the letter *M*?
>
> **Sue:** OK. I'll buy you a magazine. Hartmut, will you buy me something that begins with the letter *P*?

Activity 3

How do people request permission to speak with someone on the telephone? Are these ways different depending on the situation?

Make at least five observations to complete the following chart. If you cannot make direct observations, you can interview people about what they say in different situations.

Setting	Relationship	What They Say

Activity 4

Congratulations! You have just won a gift certificate for Easy–Does–It Maid Services. This entitles you to four hours of maid service for your home. First, make a list of what you want the maid to do in your home (clean your windows, do your laundry, scrub the toilet, etc.). Then, write these requests on a polite note to your "maid."

U N I T

16

Past Habitual

Used To with *Still* and *Anymore*, Adverbs of Frequency

Task

Work with several other students. Look at the photographs of these well-known people as they look today. If you are not sure who all these people are or why they are famous, try to find someone in the class who does.

Meryl Streep

Madonna

Diana Ross

Bruce Springsteen

Tina Turner

Warren Beatty

Look at the photographs of the same people. These photographs all came from their high school yearbooks. Match the old photographs with the current ones.

In your opinion, who has changed the most? Who has changed the least? Why do you think so?

Photographs from: *Yearbook, The Most Star-studded Graduating Class* by the Editors of *Memories Magazine*. Copyright 1990 by Diamandis Communications, Inc. Used by permission of Doubleday, a division of Bantam Doubleday Dell Publishing Group, Inc.

Focus 1

Comparing Past and Present with *Used To*

MEANING

- *Used to* shows that something was true or regularly happened in the past, but it does not happen now in the present:

    Tina Turner **used to** have short, wavy hair (but now she doesn't).

Focus 2

FORM

Used To

FORM

- *Used to* does not change form to agree with the subject:

Statement	Negative	Question
I You We They } used to work.	I You We They } did not use to work. (didn't)	Did { I you we they } use to work?
She He It } used to work.	She He It } did not use to work. (didn't)	Did { she he it } use to work?

Exercise 1

Make statements with *used to* about the changes in Madonna and Bruce Springsteen. Use the words in parentheses. You can add other ideas of your own.

1. Madonna

   a. (have a big nose) *She used to have a bigger nose; she didn't use to have a small one.*

   b. (be a dancer) _____ .

   c. (be poor) _____ .

   d. (live in Michigan) _____ .

2. Bruce Springsteen

   a. (have straight hair) _____ .

   b. (play football in high school) _____ .

   c. (live in New Jersey) _____ .

   d. (sing about blue-collar life) _____ .

Focus 3

MEANING

Anymore

MEANING

- *Anymore* shows a change in a situation or activity that was regular or habitual in the past:

Past	Present

   (a) Madonna used to live in Michigan, but she doesn't live there anymore.

- It is not necessary to repeat the second verb phrase if it is the same as the first one:

   (b) Madonna used to live in Michigan, but she doesn't anymore.

- You can also use *anymore* without *used to*:

   (c) Madonna doesn't live in Michigan anymore.
   (From this sentence, we understand that she used to live there.)

Focus 4

Position of *Anymore*

FORM

- *Anymore* comes at the end of the sentence or clause:
  - **(a)** I don't live in Brazil **anymore.**
  - **(b)** They don't work here **anymore**.
  - **(c)** Alice doesn't live here **anymore.**
- *Anymore* is always used with a negative:
  - **(d)** We don't go there **anymore.**
  - **(e)** They never talk to me **anymore.**
  - **(f)** No one likes him **anymore.**

Exercise 2

Rewrite the statements you wrote in Exercise 1, using *anymore* and *used to* if appropriate. (The conjunction *but* may be helpful in these statements.)

> **EXAMPLE:** *Madonna doesn't have black hair anymore.*
> *Madonna used to have black hair, but she doesn't anymore.*

Focus 5

MEANING

Still

MEANING

- To show that someone or something has NOT changed, you can use *still*.
  - **(a)** She lived in New Mexico 15 years ago; she lives in New Mexico now:
    She **still** lives in New Mexico.
- *Still* means that the action or habit continues to the time of speaking.
  - **(b)** He smoked 20 cigarettes a day in the past; he smokes 20 cigarettes a day now:
    He **still** smokes 20 cigarettes a day.
    (From this sentence, we understand that he started this habit in the past and hasn't stopped.)

181

Focus 6

Position of *Still*

- *Still* is a mid-sentence adverb. It comes:
  - **before the main verb:**
    - **(a)** He **still** lives in New Orleans.
  - **after the verb *be* or an auxiliary verb:**
    - **(b)** He is **still** crazy after all these years.
    - **(c)** I will **still** love you.

Exercise 3

Look back at the Task. Write statements using *still* about the people who you think have not changed very much. Use the words in parentheses, but also add other ideas of your own.

1. Meryl Streep

   a. (long, blond hair) _____ .

   b. (very slim) _____ .

2. Bruce Springsteen

   a. (house in New Jersey) _____ .

   b. (called The Boss) _____ .

Can you add anything else you know about these people? Now write about Diana Ross, Warren Beatty, and Tina Turner, showing how they have or have not changed. Use *still, anymore* or *used to* in your descriptions.

Exercise 4

Complete the following with *still* or *anymore* as appropriate.

1. **A**: Where's Jeff?

   B: He doesn't live here _____.

2. **A**: Is Gary home yet?

   B: No, he is _____ working.

3. **A**: Have you finished writing your book?

   B: No, I'm _____ working on it.

4. **A**: Do you want a cigarette?

   B: No, thanks, I don't smoke _____.

5. **A**: Where do you live?

   B: I _____ live at home with my parents.

6. **A**: Hurry up! We're going to be late!

   B: I'm _____ wrapping the gift.

7. **A**: How's your grandfather?

   B: He's doing pretty well, even though he can't go out much _____.

Exercise 5

Look at the maps of the island nation of Madalia. Work with a partner and use the information from the maps to complete the report below. Use *used to; didn't use to; still* and *anymore* as appropriate. Use the verbs in parentheses. The first one has been done for you as an example.

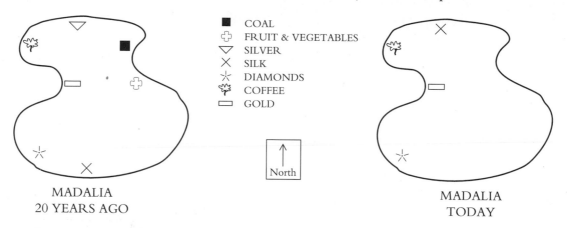

MADALIA
20 YEARS AGO

COAL
FRUIT & VEGETABLES
SILVER
SILK
DIAMONDS
COFFEE
GOLD

North

MADALIA
TODAY

EXAMPLE: Madalia is a small country that is rich in natural resources, and Madalians have exploited those resources for many years. However, in the last 20 years it is possible to note some changes in these resources. For example, 20 years ago, Madalians (1)*used to mine* (mine) *coal* in the Northeast.

In addition, they (2) _____ (grow) _____ in the East. Also, they

(3) _____ (mine) _____, but today, they (4) _____ (not)

it _____ . Furthermore, in the past, they (5) _____ (not+produce)

_____ in the North; they (6) _____ (produce) it in the

_____ . On the other hand, some things have not changed. They (7) _____

(mine) _____ in the Southwest, and they (8) _____ (grow) _____

in the Northwest. Finally, they (9) _____ (mine) _____ in the West.

Exercise 6

Look at the words below. Arrange them as a list with *most frequent* at the top and *least frequent* at the bottom. Add any other similar words you can think of and put them in the appropriate place on the list.

often	always	never	seldom
sometimes	hardly ever	usually	rarely

Check your answers with Unit 1, Focus 3.

Focus 7

Position of Adverbs of Frequency

FORM

- Unit 1 showed how adverbs of frequency come **before** the main verb: **(a)** I usually get up at six and **after** the verb *be*: **(b)** They were rarely happy.
- Adverbs of frequency are also placed:
  - **Between an auxiliary verb and the main verb:**
    - **(c)** You will **sometimes** hear from them.
    - **(d)** I have **seldom** spoken to her.
  - **Before *used to*:**
    - **(e)** They **never** used to smoke.
    - **(f)** He **always** used to call her.

Exercise 7

Write a short article for your old high school magazine, reporting on your life and habits and how they have changed (or not) over the years since you left high school. Also describe your present life and habits and compare these with your past.

Try to include the following:

something you used to do but don't do anymore

something you used to do and still do

something you didn't use to do but do now

something you never do

something you seldom do

something you sometimes do

something you often do

something you usually do

Don't forget to include changes (or not) in your physical appearance. We have begun the article for you:

I left high school in _____ (year). As I look back on my life since then, I realize that some things have changed, and some things have stayed the same. Let me start by telling you about some of the changes. . . .

Activities

Activity 1

If possible, find an old photograph of yourself (as a baby, a child, or one taken several years ago). If you cannot find a photograph, draw a picture. Stick the photo or picture to a large piece of paper and write several statements about yourself, showing things you used to do and don't do now; things you didn't use to do and things you still do. Do not write your name on the paper. Your teacher will display all the pictures and descriptions. Work with a partner and try to guess the identity of each person. Who has changed the most in the class and who has changed the least?

Activity 2

Think of a place you know well—the place where you were born or where you grew up. Write about the ways it has changed and the ways it has not changed.

Activity 3

Interview a senior citizen. Find out about changes in the world or in customs and habits during his or her lifetime. What does she or he think about these changes? Report on your findings to the class.

Activity 4

The women's movement has helped change the lives of many women in different parts of the world. However, some people argue that things have not really changed and many things are still the same for most women. Think about women's lives and roles in your mother's generation and the lives of women today. Report on what has changed and what has stayed the same.

Activity 5

Create a new identity.

This activity gives you the opportunity to "become" a different person. Choose a new identity for yourself:

What is this person's name, age, sex, profession, habits, occupation, personality, and appearance? How does this new person differ from the "real" you?

Create a full description of this person and introduce the "new" you to the class, comparing him/her with the person you used to be. If you want to, make a mask or drawing to represent the "new" you.

> **EXAMPLE:** I want to introduce the new me. I used to be a mother and a housewife, but now I am a secret agent. I never used to leave home, but now I often travel to distant and exotic places. I used to wear practical clothes that I always bought on sale. Now I usually wear black leather jumpsuits, dark glasses, and big hats, but sometimes I wear elegant evening dresses and expensive jewelry....

Activity 6

It is your job to write a profile of one of your classmates. Interview someone and find out something that your classmate:

1. never does
2. seldom does
3. sometimes does
4. often does
5. usually does
6. always does

   When you have found this information, write a report on your findings, **without using your classmate's name**. Begin with an introduction; for example, "I am going to tell you some things about one of our classmates." End your report with a question: "Can you guess who this is?"

   Display your report, along with all the other reports your classmates write. Can you identify the people described?

17

Past Perfect and
Before and *After*

Task

Work with a partner and look at Family Tree A. It shows Tom's family when he left home to travel around the world for many years.   (m) = married

A. THE BURTON FAMILY TREE: When Tom left home

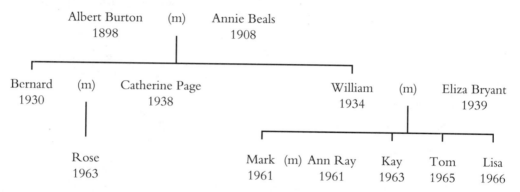

Now look at Family Tree B. It shows Tom's family after he returned home. How many differences can you find in his family between when he left and when he returned?

B. THE BURTON FAMILY TREE: When Tom returned home

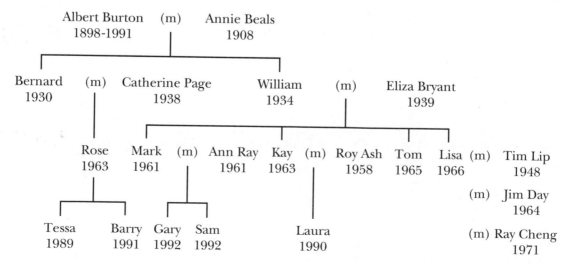

Number of differences: _____

According to the information in the family tree, how many of the following statements are true?

1. When Tom returned, his grandfather died.
2. Tom returned before his grandfather died.
3. Tom returned after his grandfather died.
4. When Tom returned, his grandfather had died.

Focus 1

MEANING

Past Perfect and Simple Past

MEANING

- When two actions or events both happened in the past, the past perfect describes the action or event which happened **first**; the simple past describes the action or event which happened **second**:

  (a) When I got there, he had eaten all the cookies. = **First**, he ate the cookies; **then**,
          2   1   I got there. (I didn't see him
                                                eat the cookies!)

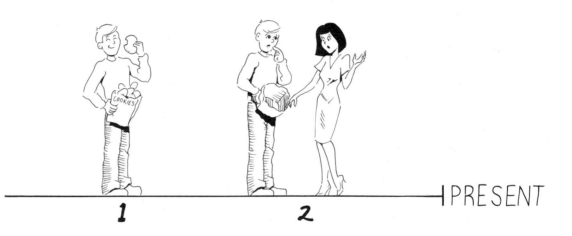

Focus 2

How to Form Past Perfect

FORM

- *had* + past participle

Statement	Negative	Question	Short Answer
I You We They } **had** arrived. ('d)	I You We They } **had not** arrived. (**hadn't**)	**Had** { I you we they } arrived?	Yes, we **had**.
She He It } **had** arrived. ('d)	She He It } **had not** arrived. (**hadn't**)	**Had** { she he it } arrived?	No, she **had not** (**hadn't**).

Exercise 1

Complete the following statements based on the family tree in the Task. Try to be as precise as possible. Use the past perfect as necessary; you can use any appropriate verb, except in the sentences where we have shown the verb to use in parentheses. The first one has been done for you.

EXAMPLE: 1. When he returned home, Tom found that his grandfather *had died* _____.

2. When Tom returned, his cousin _____ .

3. Tom arrived home to find that his sister Lisa _____ .

4. When _____ , his sister Kay _____ ;

in addition, she and her husband _____ .

5. On his return home, Tom found that his brother and sister-in-law _____

_____ .

6. When Annie Beals saw her favorite grandson, Tom, again, she had experienced both sorrow and joy. On the one hand, her _____ ; but on the other hand, she (gain) _____ .

7. Sam and Gary have never met their grandfather, because he _____ when they

_____ .

8. When Tom left home, he didn't have any _____ or nieces; when he got home, he had _____ and two _____ .

9. By the time Tom got back home, his parents and his aunt and uncle (become) _____

_____ .

10. Tom also found that Rose _____ children, but she (not) _____ .

Lisa, on the other hand, _____ three times, but she (not) _____

any children.

Exercise 2

In the following pairs of statements, decide which event probably happened first. Write *1* beside the event you think happened first and *2* beside the one you think happened second. The first one has been done for you.

EXAMPLE: My legs ached. *2*
I played tennis. *1*

1. His car broke down.
   He took the bus.

2. Charlotte was depressed.
   She failed her English exam.

3. Tanya sat in the sun all afternoon.
   Her skin was very red.

4. We didn't eat all day.
   We were really hungry.

5. Brenda's clothes were too tight.
   She didn't exercise for several months.

6. Neville couldn't sleep.
   He drank several cups of very strong coffee.

7. We studied hard for three weeks.
   We thought the test was easy.

8. The brothers fell asleep immediately.
   They played soccer for several hours.

Now join the two statements to make one sentence, using *because* to connect them; change one of the verbs in each sentence into past perfect. The first one has been done for you.

EXAMPLE: My legs ached. *2*
I played tennis. *1*
My legs ached because I had played tennis.

Focus 3

Before, After, By, and *By the Time*

MEANING

- *Before, after, by*, and *by the time* show the order of actions or events:
  - *Before* introduces the event that happened second or more recently:

First Event		Second Event
(a) They were married	**before**	Christmas.
(b) She left	**before**	I arrived.

  - *After* introduces the event that happened first:

Second Event		First Event
(c) They were married	**after**	Christmas.
(d) She left	**after**	I arrived.

- When we use *before* and *after*, it is **not necessary** to use the past perfect because they make the order of events clear:

  (e) He **left before** I got there.

  It is possible to use the past perfect in this sentence, but it is not necessary:

  (f) He **had left before** I got there.

- *By* (+ noun phrase) and *by the time* (+ verb phrase) introduce an event that happened sometime before the second or more recent event:

First Event		Second Event
(g) They were married	**by**	Christmas.
(h) She had left	**by the time**	I got there.

- *By the time* is often associated with the past perfect.
- See Unit 4, Focus 4 for punctuation rules in time clauses.

192

Exercise 3

Look at the following statements; each one uses past perfect. Check (✔) the sentences where it is necessary to use past perfect to indicate the order of events.

1. My sister graduated from college after she had gotten married.
2. I didn't see Brad last night because he had left when I got there.
3. After I had finished my work, I took a long, hot bath.
4. Kozue had checked the gas before she started to drive to Houston.
5. When the party was over, they had drunk nine bottles of wine.
6. The teacher sent the student home before the class had ended.
7. The store had closed when I got there.
8. We didn't see the movie because it had started before we got to the movie theater.
9. Cathy never knew her grandparents because they had died before she was born.
10. When Shirley got to the library, she found that someone had borrowed the book she needed.

Exercise 4

Rewrite the following sentences by omitting the underlined words and using the word in parentheses. Underline the verb in each sentence where it is possible (but not always necessary) to use past perfect. The first one has been done for you.

EXAMPLE: First Sue listened to the weather report and then she decided to go for a bike ride. (after)

After Sue listened to the weather report, she decided to go for a bike ride.

OR *Sue decided to go for a bike ride after she listened to the weather report.*

1. Sue studied several maps, and then she decided on an interesting route for her bike ride. (before)
2. She changed her clothes, and then she checked the tires on her bike. (after)
3. She put fresh water in her water bottle, and next she left home. (before)
4. She rode for several miles, then she came to a very steep hill. (after)
5. She climbed to the top of the hill, and then she stopped to drink some water and enjoy the view. (before)
6. She continued for ten more miles, and then she got a flat tire. (after)
7. She fixed the flat tire quickly, and then she continued her ride. (before)
8. It started to rain, and then she decided to go home. (after)
9. Before she got home, she rode over 30 miles. (by the time)
10. She took a long, hot shower, and finally she ate a huge plate of pasta. (after)

Focus 4

Past Perfect versus
Present Perfect

USE

- The past perfect contrasts two actions or events in the past.

  (a) She **was** tired yesterday because she **had taken** a long bike ride.

- The present perfect connects the past with the present. It tells us that something happened sometime before now (see Unit 12) or that something started in the past and continues until now (see Unit 11).

  (b) She **is** tired **now** because she **has taken** a long bike ride.

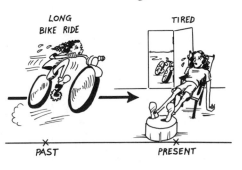

Exercise 5

Underline the mistakes in the following sentences and correct as necessary.

had

EXAMPLE: I wasn't tired yesterday because I <u>have</u> slept for ten hours the night before.

1. Nigel wasn't hungry last night because he has eaten a large fresh salmon for lunch.

2. Jan is really confused in class last Tuesday because she hadn't read the assignment.

3. Graham had gone home because he has a terrible headache today.

4. Howard is a lucky man because he had traveled all over the world.

5. Martha went to the hospital after she has broken her leg.

6. Before he has left the house, George locked all the doors and windows.

7. Professor Westerfield always returns our papers after she had graded them.

8. I didn't see you at the airport last night because your plane has left before I got there.

9. Matthew and James were late because they have missed the bus.

Exercise 6

In the story below, use the appropriate verb tense (simple past, past progressive, past perfect, present perfect) for the verbs in parentheses.

Some people attend all their high school reunions, but Al (1) _____ (go + not) back to his high school since he (2) _____ (graduate) ten years ago. Five years ago, he (3) _____ (make) arrangements to go to his five-year high school reunion, but two days before that reunion he (4) _____ (break) his leg. He (5) _____ (paint) his house on a tall ladder when he (6) _____ (lose) his balance. So he (7) _____ (not+go) to his five-year reunion.

Al (8) _____ (not+visit) his hometown for ten years and his new wife, Marta, (9) _____ (never+be) there. Al and Marta (10) _____ (get) married about a year and a half ago and they (11) _____ (not+be) married long when some of Al's high school friends (12) _____ (come) to visit them last year. So at least Marta (13) _____ (meet) a few of Al's old friends, even though she (14) _____ (not + be) to his hometown.

Activities

Activity 1

The purpose of this activity is to compare different events and achievements at different times in our lives. You will need to get information from five of your classmates to complete this.

   The left-hand column in the chart below shows different ages; your job is to find three interesting or surprising things your classmates had done by the time they reached this age. If you don't want to talk about your life, feel free to invent things that you had done at those ages. Be ready to report on your findings.

	(Name)	(Name)	(Name)	(Name)	(Name)
By the time, she or he was 5 years old . . .					
By the time she or he was 10 years old . . .					
By the time she or he was 15 years old . . .					
By the time she or he was 18 years old . . .					
By the time . . . . . . *					
By the time . . . . . . *					

* you choose an age

   Now choose *the three most surprising* pieces of information you found for *each age* (for example: The age of 15 is very interesting! By the time Roberto, Ali, and Tina were 15, they had done quite different things. Roberto had worked in his father's office, Ali had visited ten different countries, and Tina had won several prizes for swimming. . . .) Present this information as an oral or written report. Be sure to announce your purpose in an introductory sentence and to end with a concluding comment.

   If you prefer, you can turn your information into a poster presentation. Take a large poster-sized sheet of paper or card and use this to make a poster that communicates the information you found. You can use graphics, pictures, and diagrams to make your poster interesting and eye-catching. Display your poster so that your classmates can enjoy it and be ready to answer any questions they might have about it.

Activity 2
Guess Who I Was

Work in teams. With your team, choose three famous people who are now dead. Make sure you choose famous people everyone has heard of. For each person, write three statements about what s/he had done before they died. Most people should be able to guess the identity of your person after they hear all three statements.

Team A presents the first statement about their first person. The other teams have to try to guess the identity of the dead person from the statements.

Each team can ask two yes/no questions after each statement. (The "trick" is to make your statements difficult, but not impossible!)

> **EXAMPLE:** Before she died, she had made several movies.
> She had had some famous husbands and some famous lovers.
> Some people believe she had been depressed before she died.
> (Marilyn Monroe)

Activity 3

The purpose of this activity is to compare and contrast important historical events in the development of different countries.

Use the chart below to record THREE events that you think were important in the history of your country (or of a country that you know about). Don't worry if you don't know the exact date. Just mark on the chart more or less when you think it happened.

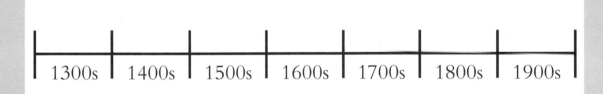

Now go around the class comparing your chart with your classmates' charts. Add to your chart significant dates from at least three other students. Where possible, try to get information from students who come from different countries. Can you add any important events from North American history too?

Use the information on your chart to compare and contrast what had happened in one country (or countries) when something else happened in another country. In addition, try to find different events that occurred at the same time in different countries. Present your findings as a written or oral report; don't forget to include an introduction and a conclusion. If you choose to make a written report, read the report carefully when you finish writing and check that you have chosen the most appropriate tenses. If you choose to make an oral report, record your presentation and afterward listen to yourself, checking specifically on your use of tenses. If you prefer, you can share your findings as a poster presentation (see Activity 1).

Quantity Classifiers with Food Items

Task

Jim has been invited to a potluck dinner (a meal where each guest brings a dish). The hostess has asked him to bring a salad for six people and some cookies. Jim wants to make everything himself and has asked for your advice and assistance. He has got the following ingredients in his kitchen; can you help him decide which ones he can use in each dish? Write them in the appropriate boxes below.

INGREDIENTS

| mustard | sugar | salt | lettuce | hard-boiled eggs | cheese | vinegar |
| chocolate chips | tomatoes | flour | olive oil | butter | eggs | garlic |

Salad	Salad Dressing	Chocolate Chip Cookies

Jim has no idea how much of each ingredient he should use. Can you help him? Write an appropriate amount beside each ingredient. Remember, there will be six people at the party.

Are there any *other* ingredients you would include? Add them to the boxes above, with suggested amounts.

MEANING

Measure Words and Expressions

MEANING

- There are some very specific ways of counting and measuring food items. Some measure expressions refer to the **portions** or **containers** or to the **weights** and **measurements** used to quantify food. Other measure words refer to the **shapes** or **typical states** in which some food items (especially certain fruits and vegetables) can be found:

CONTAINERS

"Container" words usually describe food items as we buy them in a store:

a bottle of (beer, wine)　　　　a jar of (peanut butter, mustard)

a box of (crackers, cereal)　　　a bag of (potato chips, flour)

a carton of (milk, eggs)　　　　a can of (tuna fish, beer)

PORTIONS

"Portion" words usually describe items as we find them on a plate when we eat them:

a slice of (bread)

a scoop of ice cream

a piece of (candy, cake)

a pat of butter

MEASUREMENTS

In North America, these measurement words are common in recipes:

a cup (of rice, water, flour)

a tablespoon (of salt, sugar, water)

a teaspoon (of salt, sugar, water)

a pinch (of pepper, salt)

1 teaspoon (tsp) = approximately 5 milliliters
1 tablespoon (tbs) = approximately 15 milliliters
1 cup = approximately 1/4 liter
A pinch = a *very small* amount

- Many food items (meat, vegetables, cheese) are measured in pounds (lbs) and ounces (oz).
1 ounce (oz) = approximately 30 grams
1 pound (lb) = approximately 454 grams

- Some liquids (milk, whipping cream) are measured in pints, quarts, and gallons:
1 pint = .4732 liters
1 quart = .9463 liters
1 gallon = 3.785 liters

SHAPES AND TYPICAL STATES

These expressions refer to the appearance or shape of specific items. (For example, cabbage grows in a shape similar to a "head"; therefore, we often say, "a head of cabbage.")

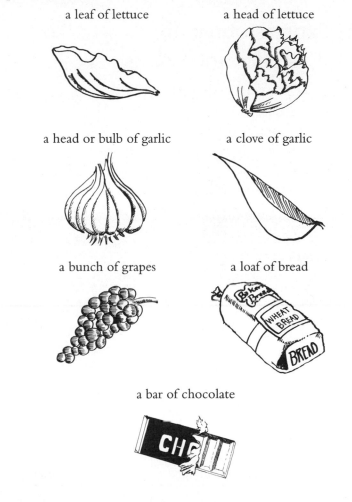

a leaf of lettuce   a head of lettuce

a head or bulb of garlic   a clove of garlic

a bunch of grapes   a loaf of bread

a bar of chocolate

Exercise 1

Turn back to the Task. Review the words you used to describe the amount of each ingredient and change them as necessary.

Exercise 2

Turn back to the Task and look carefully at the ingredients. Some of these are count nouns (tomatoes) and some are non-count nouns (flour). Write *C* beside each count noun and *NC* beside each non-count noun.

Focus 2

Measure Expressions with Count and Non-count Nouns

FORM

- Measure expressions help us to be more specific about quantity. They also enable us to make non-count nouns countable:

Three bottles of wine

Three cartons of milk

Two scoops of ice cream

Six pounds of coffee

- Most measure expressions follow this pattern:

A/An/One Two Three	+	Measure Word (Singular/Plural)	+	of	+	Noun (Non-Count/ Plural)
a		cup		of		milk
a		pound		of		apples
two		cups		of		milk
two		pounds		of		apples

- Exception: specific numbers (including *dozen*):

    a dozen eggs   ten strawberries

        NOT: a dozen of eggs

Exercise 3

These are the recipes that Jim finally used. Complete the missing parts. (The picture may help you.)

DUANE GILLOGLY

A. Jim's Super Salad

1 large _____ of red leaf lettuce

1 medium-sized _____ of romaine lettuce

1 _____ of watercress

1 large cucumber, cut into _____

6 tomatoes, cut into quarters

1/2 _____ of Swiss cheese, cut into small strips

1 _____ cooked chicken, shredded into small pieces

1/2 _____ olives

2 hard-boiled eggs, shelled and cut into quarters

1. Line a large salad bowl with the red leaf lettuce leaves.
2. Tear the romaine lettuce leaves into medium-sized pieces.
3. Place in the bowl in layers, with the watercress, slices of cucumber and tomato, cheese, and chicken.
4. Garnish with olives and eggs. Cover and refrigerate for one hour. Toss with Jim's Super Salad Dressing just before serving.

B. Jim's Super Salad Dressing

1 _____ Dijon mustard

4 _____ red wine vinegar

1 _____ sugar

1/2 _____ salt

1/2 _____ pepper

1/2 _____ olive oil

1. Put the mustard into a bowl. Whisk in vinegar, sugar, salt, and pepper.
2. Slowly add the oil while continuing to whisk the mixture.

C. Jim's Granny's Old Time Chocolate Chip Cookies

1/2 _____ butter

1 _____ brown sugar

3/4 _____ granulated sugar

2 eggs

2 _____ flour

1 _____ baking soda

1 _____ vanilla extract

1 _____ salt

1 1/2 _____ chocolate chips

1. Preheat the oven to 350° F. Grease a cookie sheet.
2. Cream the butter and both the sugars together until light and fluffy. Add the eggs and vanilla and mix well.
3. Sift the flour, baking soda, and salt. Mix thoroughly.
4. Add the chocolate chips.
5. Form into cookies. Place on a cookie tray and put on the middle rack of the oven for 8–10 minutes.
6. Cool for 5 minutes.
7. Enjoy! (This recipe makes about 40 cookies.)

Turn back to the Task and look at the ingredients (and the amounts) you suggested for these dishes. How many differences can you find between your suggestions and Jim's recipes? Whose recipe do you think will taste better?

Exercise 4

Thomas is a chef at Legends Celebrity Diner, where each item on the menu is named for a famous person. Thomas has had to take the afternoon off and has asked you to substitute for him. He has left you detailed instructions about how to make some of the most popular items on the menu. Unfortunately, some of the instructions have gotten jumbled up. Can you sort them out? Write the ingredients under the appropriate heading.

ARNOLD'S
"TERMINATOR" BURGER

_____

_____

_____

_____

_____

STING'S
"WHOLE EARTH" SANDWICH

_____

_____

_____

_____

_____

_____

TINA TURNER'S
HOT FUDGE SUNDAE

_____

_____

_____

_____

MARILYN MONROE'S
ICE-CREAM SHAKE

_____

_____

_____

_____

2 slices of whole wheat bread

2 scoops of chocolate ice cream

1/2 lb of chopped steak (cooked rare)

6 spinach leaves

2 1/2 cups of hot fudge sauce

3 slices of avocado

a dozen strawberries

2 tbs of all-natural mayonnaise

1 1/2 cups of bean sprouts

3 tbs of hot mustard

2 cups of toasted almonds

1 cup of hot chili sauce

3 scoops of vanilla ice cream

1 white hamburger bun

6 tbs of whipped cream

1 scoop of strawberry ice cream

2 cups of onion rings

1 scoop of coffee ice cream

3 crisp lettuce leaves

1 sliced tomato

Exercise 5

Two friends went shopping for a big party. They made a list of some of their favorite foods, and then they went to Food Giant, the big supermarket nearby. Here's their list.

Add the measure words (and a plural if necessary). Different answers are possible, and some answers may not require measure words.

1 1/2 _____ ground beef		2 _____ wine	
3 _____ bread		2 _____ corn chip	
2 _____ orange		2 _____ tomato	
2 _____ cheese		3 _____ ice cream	
1 _____ milk		6 _____ coke	

Exercise 6

Last week Matthew ate a delicious spaghetti sauce at his friend Nancy's house. He enjoyed it so much that Nancy lent him the recipe so that he could make a copy of it. However, Nancy has obviously used this recipe many times and it is quite difficult to read. Can you help Matthew figure out the recipe? Fill in the missing parts below.

Spaghetti Sauce

(from Nancy's kitchen)

First, cut 3 _____ of bacon into small pieces and cook over a very low heat. Stir in 1/2 _____ of ground meat along with 4 _____ garlic and 2 _____ onion, chopped up very finely. Add 1 _____ salt, a pinch of cayenne pepper and 2 _____ of fresh herbs. Mix in two 8-ounce _____ tomato sauce. Let it cook on low heat for about 30 minutes. Serve over fresh pasta.

If you were making this recipe yourself, would you change or add anything? Share any changes or additions with your classmates. Try to be as precise as possible.

Activities

Activity 1

Below is a blank Bingo card. Your teacher will read a list of food items that each require a measure word. When you hear the food item, write the measure word for that item in a box—*any* box. For example, if your teacher says "bread," you can write *slice* or *loaf* in a box. Don't start in the upper left corner; fill your boxes in any order you want. Your card should look different from your classmates'.

How to Play

When everyone has filled in their boxes, your teacher will read a food item. Write the item in a box with a matching measure word. For example, if your teacher says "bread," you will write *bread* in the box that says *loaf* or *slice*. Sometimes it may be possible to write one food item in more than one box. When this happens, *choose only one box*.

When you complete a line (diagonally, vertically, or horizontally) call out "Bingo." The first person to correctly fill a line and call out "Bingo" wins the game. Good luck!

Exercise 5,6 Activity 1: Idea by Wendy Asplin

Activity 2

In Exercise 4, you saw some of the items on the menu at Legends Celebrity Diner. Get together with a classmate and create some new items for the menu at this diner. Choose three people that you think everyone in the class will know (for example, movie stars, singers, politicians, your classmates, etc.). Create a dish named for this person. Be precise about the quantity of each ingredient in the dish. Share your "dishes" with the rest of the class.

Activity 3

The purpose of this activity is to do some research about various dishes and their recipes. The dishes below are very popular in North America, but different people sometimes have quite different recipes for the same dish. Your goal is to discover some of these variations.

Brownies   Potato Salad   Cheesecake   Cranberry Sauce

Divide into groups and choose **one** of these dishes. (If you prefer, you can select a dish that isn't on this list, preferably one that you don't know how to make.) Interview several different native speakers by asking them to tell you how to make the dish you have chosen. If possible, tape-record your interview. Get together with your group and compare the directions you have gathered. How many differences can you find? Be ready to share your findings with the rest of the class.

Activity 4

This "recipe" was written by an English teacher:

"Recipe" for the Perfect Student
Ingredients:
1 cup of motivation
1 cup of determination
1/2 cup of patience
1/2 cup of tolerance
1 cup of laughter
1 cup of imagination
1 1/2 cups of willingness to make a guess
1 cup of independence
1 1/2 cups of cooperation with others
1 pinch of fun
Combine ingredients and stir gently to bring out the best flavor.

What do you think the teacher means by this?

Get together with a partner and create a "recipe" of your own. Here are some ideas, but you probably have plenty of your own:

Recipe for a long-lasting marriage
Recipe for the perfect boyfriend/girlfriend/husband/wife
Recipe for the perfect teacher
Recipe for the perfect house
Recipe for the perfect mother/father

Share your recipes with the rest of the class.

Activity 5

Your class has been given $5 per person to spend on food and drink for a party. Divide into groups and draw up a list showing how you will spend this money. Be specific about the quantities you will buy.

Activity 6

Think of your favorite recipe, preferably a typical dish from your country. Write it on a piece of paper and give it to your teacher. Your teacher will distribute the recipes among the class so that everyone receives somebody else's recipe. Try to cook the recipe according to the instructions you were given. Bring the results to class.

Activity 7

Organize an international potluck. Everyone in the class should prepare a dish, preferably from his/her country. Bring the dish to class to share and enjoy with your classmates. Be ready to tell your classmates how to make your dish. If possible, try to arrange your potluck at somebody's house, so you can watch each other cook. After the meal, collect all the recipes for an international cookbook. Make copies and distribute them to the class.

19

Articles
Definite, Indefinite, and ∅

Task

Put the following sentences in order so that they make a logical story. When you have finished, check to see if other students have the story in the same order.

a. Esinam found a real-estate agent to help them.

b. They finally decided to buy the house, remodel the kitchen, and take out the old kitchen cabinets.

c. Even though the house was little, it had a big, old-fashioned kitchen and two bathrooms.

d. Next they viewed a pretty house by a lake, but the house was too expensive.

e. Finally they saw a little house at the end of a dead-end street.

f. When I last talked to them, they were happy with their decision, and they liked the house a lot.

g. Esinam and Stuart decided to buy a house.

h. The real-estate agent then showed them a house near some apartment buildings, but the house was too big, and the apartment buildings were too ugly.

i. The little house was just right—not too expensive, not too far away from work, not too big.

j. First they looked at a nice house in the suburbs, but the house was too far away from work.

k. They told the real-estate agent that they wanted to live in a quiet neighborhood. They also said that they preferred small houses.

Focus 1

Articles

FORM
MEANING

- There are four articles in English, one definite and three indefinite forms.

  DEFINITE
  - *The* is used with specific nouns. Nouns are specific when the listener knows what specific thing or person the speaker is talking about.

    (a) Father to son: Where did you park **the** car?

  INDEFINITE
  - *A* (or *an* before nouns that start with a vowel sound) is used with singular count nouns that are non-specific.

    (b) I need **a** new car.
  - *Some* is used for plural count and non-count nouns that are indefinite.

    (c) I need **some** pencils.

    (d) Would you like **some** rice?
  - Ø is used for plural count and non-count nouns that are indefinite and when the speaker wishes to talk about things in general.

    (e) Pencils are made with lead.

    (f) Rice is eaten in Africa.

Focus 2

The Definite Article: Second Mention

USE

- *The* is used when the listener knows what specific thing or person the speaker is talking about. The speaker is thinking, "you know what I mean" when he or she uses *the*.
- The speaker thinks that the listener knows what she or he means in different situations:
  - when the noun has already been mentioned = second mention

    (a) She used to have a cat and a dog, but **the** cat got run over.
- when a related noun has already been mentioned, it is called related second mention

    (b) He bought a suit yesterday, but **the** jacket had a button missing, so he had to return it. (**Jacket** is part of a **suit**: the listener knows which jacket since **suit** was already mentioned.)

    (c) I had a lock but I lost **the** key for it.

Exercise 1

Underline all the uses of *the* in the statements in the Task. For each one, describe why it is used based on the rules in Focus 2 regarding second mention or related mention. If neither of these rules helps to explain why *the* is used, circle *the*. You will return to this later, in Exercise 3.

Exercise 2

Each time *the* is underlined in the sentences below, decide **why** it is used. If it is used because it is the second mention of the noun following it, circle *S* (for *Second* mention). If it used because a related noun has been mentioned, circle *R* (for *Related* mention).

1. Jerry was late for his appointment, so he went into a telephone booth near the bus stop to make a phone call. It looked like someone was living in the telephone booth.   Ⓢ R

2. There was a small blanket covering the window of the telephone booth like a curtain.   S R

3. The floor of the telephone booth was swept clean with a broom.   S R

4. The broom was hung on a little hook in the corner of the telephone booth.   S R

5. By the telephone, there was a pen and a notepad with a short list of names and telephone numbers.   S R

6. The names and telephone numbers were each written in a different color ink.   S R

7. Jerry also noticed that there was a coffee mug and a toothbrush sitting neatly by the telephone directory.   S R

8. The coffee mug looked like it had recently been rinsed. There were still drops of water in it.   S R

9. Jerry had such a strong feeling that he was in someone's living space that he decided to find another place to make the phone call.   S R

Focus 3

The Definite Article: Uniqueness

- We also use the definite article *the* when the noun is **unique**. In other words, there is **only one** possible reference because
  - the place where you are speaking makes it clear.
    - **(a)** **The** flowers are beautiful. (said in a garden)
    - **(b)** Who painted **the** ceiling? (said in a room) or
  - there's only *one* of the thing mentioned.
    - **(c)** **The** sun is shining today. (unique reference—there's only one sun) or
  - the adjectives used with the noun make only one reference possible (examples of these kinds of adjectives: *same, only, right*; numbers like *first, second, last*; and superlatives like *best, happiest, hardest*).
    - **(d)** We'll have to wait for **the** next bus. (There's only one possible next bus.)
    - **(e)** That's **the** hardest test I've ever taken. (There's only one possible hardest test.)
    - **(f)** She's **the** first person I met here and **the** only friend I have.

Exercise 3

In Exercise 1, you circled all the uses of *the* in the Task that could not be explained by either a) the second mention rule, or b) the related mention rule. For each time you circled *the*, use the rules from Focus 3 (above) to explain why *the* was used. (Make a list on a separate sheet of paper.)

Focus 2 and 3, and Exercise 3: Idea from Roger Berry, 1991, Rearticulating the articles, *ELT Journal* 45:3, 252–299.

Exercise 4

For each of the following sentences, answer the following questions:

a. Where would you hear this sentence spoken?

b. Who do you think the speaker is?

c. What do you think happened **before** or **after** the sentence was spoken? What do you think the conversation was about **before** or **after** the sentence was spoken?

Use the answers to these questions to discuss in class why *the* was used in each case.

1. Turn on *the* TV.
2. Could you change *the* channel?
3. We need some more chalk. Would you mind checking *the* blackboard in *the* back?
4. *The* rosebushes are lovely.
5. Could you pass *the* salt, please?
6. Excuse me, where's *the* women's restroom?
7. *The* sky is so blue today. I don't think you'll need *the* umbrella.
8. Have you seen *the* dog?
9. What a surprise! We live on *the* same street.

Focus 4

USE

The Indefinite Article

USE

- The indefinite article *a* (or *an* before nouns that start with a vowel sound) is used when the speaker first mentions a thing or person.
    - **(a)** I read **a** great book yesterday.
    - **(b)** Martha just bought **a** new backpack.
- It can also be used when the speaker is not talking about a specific thing or person but is making a generalization.
    - **(c)** I'd like to get **a** ticket to the concert on Friday.
    - **(d)** He is hoping to find **a** new wife.
- *Some* is used for the same purposes with plural or non-count nouns.
    - **(e)** I would like to read **some** more books.
    - **(f)** We need **some** more chalk.

214

Exercise 5

Fill in the blanks in the story below with *a/an*, *some*, or *the*.

1. Esinam and Stuart had _____ friend, Mel, who was also looking for _____ house to buy.

2. Mel was especially interested in finding _____ house with _____ view.

3. Mel thought that _____ best views were from _____ hills east of town.

4. There were _____ houses for sale in that area, but they were all very expensive.

5. Mel decided to ask for _____ loan from his parents so that he could afford to buy _____ house with his favorite view.

6. First he looked at _____ big old house with four bedrooms.

7. He liked _____ house very much, but it was too big for just one person.

8. So he decided to ask _____ friends to live with him and pay rent.

9. He bought _____ house, even though it was _____ only house he had looked at!

Exercise 6

Now look back at the completed story (Exercise 5) and tell why you used each article (*a/an*, *some*, or *the*).

Exercise 7

Fill in the blanks in the story below with *a/an*, *some*, or *the*.

1. Last fall Anita worked in _____ apple orchard, picking apples.

2. _____ work was not easy.

3. She had sore muscles _____ first week of work, and every night she slept very soundly.

4. _____ first orchard she worked in was considered small, with only 50 trees.

5. It was owned by _____ old, retired couple, who worked in the orchard as _____ hobby.

6. _____ next orchard Anita worked in seemed huge, about 20 acres.

7. In this orchard, _____ of the trees had yellow apples, which were called "Golden Delicious."

8. Every day Anita ate _____ apples for breakfast and for lunch.

9. Even though _____ weather was beautiful, and _____ hard work made her feel very healthy, Anita was relieved when _____ apple-picking season was over.

Focus 5

USE

The Ø Article

USE

• When we talk about things in general (all trees, all literature), we can use a plural noun or non-count noun with zero article (Ø).

   (a) There are many uses for trees.

   (b) Literature, art, and music are considered "the fine arts."

Exercise 8

Circle the errors in article usage in the sentences below. Specifically, should you use *the* or the zero (Ø) article?

1. The love is a very important thing in our lives.
2. Without the love, we will be lonely and confused.
3. I believe that the money is not as important as love, although some people don't feel this way.
4. If the money is too important, then we become greedy.
5. When we get old, the health becomes almost as important as love.
6. My grandmother says, "Just wait and see. Work you do and the money you earn are important now, but when you're old...
7. ...love that you feel for your family and friends, health of your loved ones—these are the things that will be most important."

Exercise 9

Fill in the blanks in the story below with *the*, zero (Ø) article, *a/an* or *some*.

1. Berta likes ___ _____ books. She has two rooms full of books in her house.

2. In general, she finds that _____ books are expensive, although _____ paperback books are still fairly inexpensive.

3. Usually _____ used books are about a third of the price of _____ new books.

4. _____ textbooks are pretty expensive.

5. _____ romance novels and _____ mysteries are usually pretty cheap.

6. _____ cheapest books of all are at Al's Second-hand Bookstore in the University District.

7. At Al's, _____ used books in the back room are all three dollars or less.

8. Once she bought _____ book that cost $75. This book was _____ atlas, with pages and pages of beautifully colored maps.

9. Berta feels that _____ books are a good thing to spend money on these days even though they might seem kind of expensive when you buy them.

10. The nicest thing about _____ books, according to Berta, is that you can always keep them, to look at or read again and again.

Activities

Activity 1

TIC-TAC-TOE/Arranging Objects—Choose a small common object that can be moved around. It can be something that you are wearing (a ring, a watch) or carrying with you (a pencil, a book). It is all right if some people choose the same object. All of you will give your objects to one student.

Form two teams. Each team will tell the student who has the objects to arrange them according to their directions, one sentence at a time. (For example, "Put a book under the ring. Put the red pencil next to the book.") If the article usage in the sentence is correct (and the person is able to follow the directions), then the team gets to put an X or O in any of the tic-tac-toe squares. If it is not correct, then the team must pass. The first team to get three X's or three O's in a row or diagonally wins the game.

Activity 2

Find a photograph or drawing to bring to class. First describe the picture, and then work together to tell the class a story about it. This will be a "chain story." The first person says one thing about the picture, the second repeats that and adds another sentence, etc., until each student has contributed at least one sentence to the story. Concentrate on using articles correctly as you compose the story orally.

Activity 3

Now without the help of your classmates, write a short description of the picture that you described in Activity 2. It doesn't have to be exactly the same as the story you made, but again, try to use the articles correctly.

Activity 4

Here are some things that people say contribute to their happiness: love, romance, success, wealth/money, fame, popularity, health, religion. Interview three people about what they think is most important for their happiness. (Tape-record people's answers, if possible.) Be sure to get information about the people you are interviewing, such as age group, gender, occupation.

Summarize the results of your interviews and see if there is agreement in people's answers.

Activity 5

Find at least four headlines in a newspaper. Copy them down or cut them out and bring them to class. Put in articles (*the*, Ø article, *a/an* or *some*) wherever you think they are appropriate, in order to make the headline into a more complete statement. (Note: You might need to add main verbs or auxiliaries too, such as a form of *be* or *do*.)

With the headlines you have chosen, is it possible to use more than one of these choices of articles? If so, does the meaning of the statement change?

> **EXAMPLE:** RIOT IN L.A. ALARMS NATION
>
> Adding articles: The riot in L.A. alarms the nation.
>
> Explanation: *The* riot is used because it is a specific riot (April 1992) that we have all heard about. It is not possible to choose another article.
>
> *The* nation is used because we all know **which** nation they are talking about; this is from a United States newspaper, so *the* nation refers to the United States. Thus, this is the only article choice that makes sense.

20

Articles with Geographical and Institutional Terms

Task

How much geographical information do your classmates know? Move around the classroom to collect information to complete the chart below. Write down all the **different** answers you get in each category. When you have spoken to five other students, decide on the correct answers. Use a recent edition of an almanac to check your answers.

WHAT IS ... ?

the largest continent in the world	
the longest river	
the largest country (in size, not population)	
the biggest island	
the highest mountain range	
the highest mountain	
the biggest desert	
the largest ocean	
the largest lake	
the largest planet	

Focus 1

Geographical Names

FORM

- Geographical names are proper nouns, and **usually** you don't need an article with them:
  (a) He lives in China.
  (b) Lake Superior is in North America.

Exercise 1

Look at the categories below. For each category (1–10), put the correct answers from the Task in either Column A or B. (Don't worry about Column C; you will complete this later.) For example, the highest mountain is **Mt. Everest**, which does not use *the*, so this would go in column B for #6.

Category	(A) Use *the*	(B) Don't Use *the*	(C) Exceptions
1. rivers	Yellow River		
2. continents		North America	
3. countries		Poland	
4. islands		Jamaica	
5. mountain ranges	Andes		
6. mountain peaks		**Mt. Everest**	
7. deserts	Gobi Desert		
8. oceans	Artic Ocean		
9. lakes		Lake Union	
10. planets		Mars	

Now check your answers with Focus 2. Can you now add more examples to each column, and can you also find some examples for Column C?

Focus 2

Articles with Geographical Names

- We do **not** use *the*:
  - With the names of
    continents (South America)
    planets (Mars) (Exception: *the* earth, which can also be simply *Earth*)
    parks (Yosemite National Park)
    streets and most highways (First Avenue, Interstate 90)
    cities
  - Before individual (rather than plural)
    islands (Jamaica)
    mountain peaks (Mt. Shasta) (Exception: the Matterhorn)
    lakes (Lake Union)
  - With the names of countries (France, Australia), **except** when they are viewed as unions or federations, as in the United Kingdom, or are plural, as in the Philippines
- We use *the*:
  - With chains or groups (plural rather than singular) of
    islands (the Hawaiian Islands)
    mountains (the Andes)
    lakes (the Great Lakes)
  - With the names of
    rivers (the Yellow River)
    deserts (the Gobi Desert)
    oceans and seas (the Arctic Ocean, the Caspian Sea)
    regions, when the direction word acts as the proper noun (the West, the Midwest; but not Southeast Asia, where the continent is named)
  - With nouns with *of* in them, such as the Republic of China, the Bay of Bengal
- Note: These are the **regular** patterns for using articles with geographical names. Occasionally you will come across other exceptions.

Exercise 2

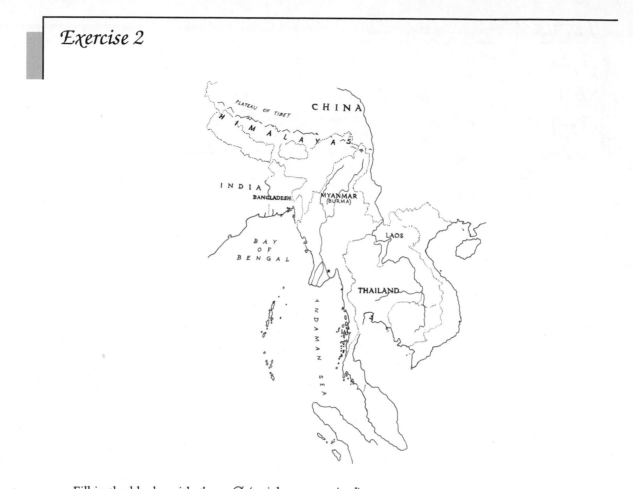

Fill in the blanks with *the* or ∅ (article not required).

(1) _____ Myanmar is sandwiched between (2) _____ India and (3) _____ Bangladesh on one side and (4) _____ China, (5) _____ Laos, and (6) _____ Thailand on the other, while to the south is (7) ___the___ Andaman Sea and (8) ___the___ Bay of Bengal. Myanmar has several important river systems including (9) ___the___ Irrawaddy, which runs almost the entire length of the country and enters the sea in a vast delta region southwest of (10) _____ Rangoon, the capital. (11) ___the___ Mekong River forms the border between Myanmar and Laos. (12) ___the___ Himalayas rise in the north of Myanmar, and (13) _____ Hkakabo Razi,

on the border between Myanmar and Tibet, is the highest mountain in (14) _____

southeast Asia, at 5881 meters (19,297 feet).

> (Adapted from *Burma, A Travel Survival Kit*, by Tony Wheeler, 1982. Lonely Planet Publications)

Now use the information from this exercise to complete the map.

Exercise 3

Look at these conversations. Underline all the geographical names, names of institutions, and names of famous buildings or places.

Dialogue 1

A: My brother is a freshman at the University of Washington.

B: Really? I thought he was at Louisiana State.

A: He was. He didn't like the climate in the South, so he decided to move to the Pacific Northwest.

Dialogue 2

A: How long did you stay in Washington, D.C.?

B: Not very long. We had just enough time to see the White House, the Capitol, and the Washington Monument.

A: Did you get to any museums or art galleries?

B: We wanted to go to the Smithsonian and the National Gallery, but we didn't have time.

A: Too bad!

In these examples, when is the definite article used and when is it *not* used? List all the examples from the conversation if that is helpful.

Focus 3

FORM

Articles with Institutional Terms

FORM

- We do **not** use *the*:
  - when the name of a university or college comes directly **before** the word *university* or *college* (Boston College), or when *university* or *college* is implied. (Louisiana State [University]).
- We do not **usually** use *the*:
  - with the names of parks (Central Park, Discovery Park).

- We use *the*:
  - when the phrase *University of* comes before the rest of the name (the University of Northern Iowa); *college of*
  - with the names of tourist attractions, monuments, or famous buildings (the Space Needle, the Golden Gate Bridge) (Exception: Disneyland);
  - with museums and libraries (the Museum of Natural History).

Exercise 4

The following conversation is between Sheryl Smith, a real-estate agent, and the Joneses, who are considering buying a house in the city of Golden Oaks. Fill in the blanks with *the* (when the definite article is required) or ∅ (when no article is required).

Sheryl Smith: I'm sure you'd like the area. It borders (1) _____ Discovery Park, which has free outdoor concerts at (2) ___~~the~~___ Rutherford Concert Hall, and also there's (3) ___the___ Whitehawk Native American Art Museum, which you've probably heard of. It's quite well known.

Mike Jones: Yes, yes.

Donna Jones: What about schools?

Sheryl Smith: Well, there's (4) ___the___ Smith College of Architecture, of course—

Donna Jones: I mean public schools. For our children.

Sheryl Smith: Oh, well, (5) ____?___ Golden Oaks Elementary School is only a few blocks away, on (6) _____ First Avenue. And there's a high school about a mile north of the park.

Mike Jones: (pointing): Aren't those (7) ___~~the~~___ White Mountains?

Sheryl Smith: Yes. On clear days, you can even see (8) _____ Mt. Wildman, the tallest mountain in the range.

Mike Jones: Oh, yes. I heard about a good fishing spot there, on (9) ___~~the~~___ Blue Lake.

Sheryl Smith: Yes, my husband goes there and to (10) ___the___ Old Man's River to fish. He could tell you all about it.

Mike Jones: Mrs. Smith, I think you might have made a sale today.

Exercise 5

Fill in the blanks with *the* or ∅ (article not required).

SAN FRANCISCO MUST SEE'S FOR FIRST-TIMERS

Once considered impossible to build, (1) _____ Golden Gate Bridge, a 1.7-mile-long single-span suspension bridge, was opened in 1937. A walk across offers a fantastic view of the city, (2) _____ Marin Headlands, and (3) _____ East Bay. Experience a taste of (4) _____ Orient in (5) _____ Chinatown, the largest Chinese settlement outside (6) _____ Asia. Originally only sand dunes, (7) _____ Golden Gate Park owes its existence to Scottish landscape architect John McLaren. In addition to the beauty of its landscape, the park contains: a conservatory modeled after (8) _____ Kew Gardens; (9) _____ Asian Art Museum with its well-known Brundage collection; (10) _____ Strybing Arboretum with its worldwide plant collection; and (11) _____ California Academy of Sciences, which includes a planetarium and aquarium.

(Adapted from *San Francisco*, TESOL Convention 1990, Leslie Reichert)

Activities

Activity 1

It is often said that North Americans do not know very much about geography, compared to people from other countries. The purpose of this activity is for non-native speaking people living in the United States (or near Americans if you are in a country other than the United States), to conduct a small survey to see to what extent this is true.

Take the questions from the Task and draw up a chart of your own. Add other items to the chart if you want. Then use this chart to get information from as many Americans as you can—ideally from five to ten different people. Compare the answers you receive with those that your classmates gave you, and share your findings with the rest of the class.

On the basis of the findings from everyone in class, is it true that Americans know less about geography than people from other countries? Are there any reasons to explain your results?

Activity 2

With the help of your teacher, form teams. Each team will have five minutes to think of as many names of islands, mountains, and lakes as possible. Each name, with correct article use, will be worth one point. The team that has the most correct names + articles wins.

Activity 3

Think of a city or region you know and like. What places are the "Must See's For First-Timers"? Write a short description of the tourist attractions and special features. If time allows, draw a map giving the relative locations of these places.

Activity 4

Rita and Ray were planning an overnight backpacking trip into the mountains, so they asked their friend Bill to give them directions to a nice camping spot where he had camped many times. Bill told Ray the directions over the phone. Below are the notes that Ray took:

Round trip — Fire Mountain — 14 miles
1 mile before Fire Mountain — Crystal Pass (great
      camping spot)
To trailhead:
north from Seattle — Interstate 5 through Mt. Vernon
east — Highway 65 to Darringtom
1 1/2 miles past Darrington left on road — Smokey Peak
      Road or Smoke Peak??
about 2 miles down road — left — parking area (Fire Mt.
      trail sign, elevation 2000 feet)
steep trail — Lake Megan (about 1 1/2 miles)
trail splits off (3 miles?) — right — across Southfork
      River — not downhill
up to Crystal Mountain (elevation 4500 feet?) and
      campsite
great view of Fire Mt.
cold, take warm clothes!

Instructions: "Translate" this note into complete directions and a description of the route to Bill's special camping spot.

UNIT

21

Indirect Objects with *For*

Task

Match the pictures to the pieces of dialogue below. Write the number of the picture beside the appropriate piece of dialogue.

A: Is this yours? You left it on that table over there.

B: Let *me* take those; they're much too heavy for you.

C: I'll pay! I insist.

D: Sit down and relax. Dinner will be ready in a few minutes.

E: Hey! Don't forget your keys! Catch!

F: I hope this is going to fit you.

Now match the description to each picture. Write the letter beside each picture.

a. She bought lunch for him.
b. He carried her books for her.
c. He cooked dinner for her.
d. She threw the keys to him.
e. He handed a wallet to her.
f. She knitted a sweater for him.

Focus 1

FORM

Direct and Indirect Objects

FORM

    (a) He wrote a letter.
        Letter is the direct object. It tells us **what** he wrote.

- Sometimes we use two objects:
    (b) He wrote a letter to his mother.
        His mother is the indirect object. It tells us **whom** he wrote to.
    (c) He cooked dinner for his wife.
        His wife is the indirect object. It tells us **whom** he cooked for.

Exercise 1

Look at sentences a–f in the Task. Underline the direct object and (circle) the indirect object in each sentence.

Focus 2

MEANING
For versus *To*

- When we use two objects, *for* and *to* add important information to the sentence:

    (a) Jim gave the books to Jean.

    To tells us about the **direction** of the action: the books went **from** Jim *to* Jean.

    (b) John cooked dinner for Betty.

    For tells us that the action **helps** and **pleases** the person who "receives" it. In this situation, John did something that helped and pleased Betty.

- We often use these verbs with *for* to show that the action helps and pleases someone else:

build	do	cook
prepare	buy	carry
clean	get	make
keep	fix	knit
save		

Exercise 2

Match Column A with Column B to complete the sentences that begin in A. The first one has been done for you.

A

Bruce cleaned the house for his neighbor

Graham made a cheesecake for Lara

They prepared a picnic for their children

Dan bought those earrings for Jane

Her friends prepared a surprise party for her

Susan built a bookshelf for her parents

Alan bought a blue scarf for his aunt

Sean fixed his sister's car for her

B

because she already had a blue dress.

because she didn't know anything about engines.

because it was her birthday.

because she was too tired to do it herself.

because they had too many books and not enough space for them.

because they wanted to eat at the beach.

because she wanted them.

because it was her favorite dessert.

Exercise 3

Read this conversation:

Barbara: Happy birthday, Joan!

Joan: Oh, Barbara! A necklace! Thank you!

Barbara: So, are you having a good birthday?

Joan: Oh, yes. The kids cooked me breakfast, and then they gave me some great presents. Joey made me a vase. He made it at school. And Julie knitted me a scarf.

Barbara: What about Jim? What did he give you?

Joan: I couldn't believe it! Jim gave me a pair of diamond earrings!

Barbara: Diamond earrings!! You're lucky. On my birthday, my husband bought me tickets to a Giants game. And I don't even like baseball!

Now complete the chart below, showing who did what for Joan on her birthday.

Joan's Birthday Treats: Who Did What For Joan on Her Birthday?

Her Son Joey	Her Daughter Julie
He made her a vose	She knitted her a scarf. They cooked her a breakfast
Her Friend Barbara	**Her Husband Jim**
A necklace	He gave her a pair of diamond earrings.

Underline the direct objects and (circle) the indirect objects in the following parts of Joan's conversation.

The kids cooked (me) breakfast.

Joey made (me) a vase.

Julie knitted (me) a scarf.

Jim gave (me) a pair of diamond earrings.

Compare these with the sentences you worked on in Exercise 1. What differences do you notice? Write down a few of them.

Focus 3

Using *For* to Highlight New Information

USE

- "The kids made me breakfast" means the same as "The kids made breakfast for me." However, when **the thing** is new information and **the person who receives it** is not, you can make these changes:

  (a) He bought me a *diamond ring*. You emphasize the **ring**, not the person who received it.

- When you think the person who received it is the more important or new information, you can use *for*:

  (b) He bought a diamond ring *for me*. You emphasize the **person** who received the ring. (not you)

- In both cases, the part of the message you want to emphasize comes last.

Focus 4

FORM

Deleting *For* = omit for

FORM

	Subject	Verb	Direct Object	Indirect Object
(a) He		bought a	diamond ring	for me.

deletion for

	Subject	Verb		Indirect Object	Direct Object
(b) He		bought a	diamond ring for (me) → He bought	me	a diamond ring.

- Omit *for* and put the indirect object **in front of** the direct object.

231

Exercise 4

Answer the following questions, using the words in parentheses. Use *for* when you think it is more important to emphasize **who** benefits from the action; omit *for* when you think it is best to emphasize **what** they receive.

EXAMPLE: 1. Who did you buy that for?

I bought it for Cathy. (Cathy)

2. What did you buy for your friend—a blouse or a sweater? _I bought her a blouse_

(a blouse)

3. Who did he build the house for? _He built the house for his mother_ (his mother)

4. Did Sue cook that for Josh or for Larry? _She cooked that for Josh_ (Josh)

5. What did she cook for him—pasta or fish? _She cooked him pasta_ (pasta)

6. Did you make that for Nina or for Chloe? _I made that for Nina_ (Nina)

7. What did you get for your sister—a book or a record? _I got her a book_

(a book)

Focus 5

FORM

Verbs That Do Not Omit *For*

FORM

- It is not possible to omit *for* and move the indirect object in front of the direct object with **all** verbs. For example, you can say:

  (a) He cooked dinner for me.   OR   He cooked me dinner.
- However, with some verbs, you can't usually omit *for*. For example, you can say:

  (b) She solved the problem for me.

    NOT: She solved me the problem.

Some Verbs That Can Omit *For*		Some Verbs That Usually Can't Omit *For*	
buy	build	explain	repair
cook	save	open	do
make	bake	carry	prepare
knit	get	fix (= repair)	solve
sew		clean	

Exercise 5

Read the following carefully. Where you think it is possible, rewrite the sentences without using *for*.

1. My suitcase was very heavy, but my friend carried it for me.

   _____ No

2. Gloria cooked a fabulous dinner for Harvey.

   _____ Yes

3. Gary was cold, so Karen knitted a scarf for him.

   _____ Yes

4. If I win the lottery, I'll buy a house by the ocean for you.

   _____ Yes

5. Chuck left his wallet at home, so Ross bought dinner for him.

   _____ Yes

6. The teacher was carrying a lot of books, so the student opened the door for him.

   _____ No -

7. On your birthday, I'll bake a cake for you.

   _____ Yes

8. George doesn't know anything about machines, so Erica always fixes his car for him.

   _____ No

Exercise 6

Read the sets of sentences below. Decide which sentences, if any, are incorrect in each set. Change any incorrect sentences to correct ones.

1. Tomorrow is my father's birthday, and . . .
   a. I'm going to get him a present.
   b. I'm going to get a present him.
   c. I'm going to get a present for him.

2. Because it's his birthday, . . .
   a. I'm also going to fix him his car.
   b. I'm also going to fix him for his car.
   c. I'm also going to fix his car for him.

3. He likes to eat and drink, so. . . .
   a. my sister is going to bake a cake him.
   b. my sister is going to bake a cake for him.
   c. my sister is going to bake him a cake.
   d. my mother is going to make him his favorite dessert.
   e. my aunt is going to cook him a special meal.
   f. my aunt is going to cook him a special meal for him.
   g. my brother is going to prepare him his favorite cocktail.
   h. I'm also going to buy him some wine.
   i. I'm also going to buy some wine for him.

Activities

Activity 1

When people have problems, they sometimes write letters to magazines or newspapers, asking for advice. Can you help solve one of these problems? Read the following letter to "Dear Arby." Then work with a partner and make a list of all the things "Confused" could do for her grandfather. Compare your ideas with those of your classmates and then complete Arby's answer.

DEAR ARBY. . . .

Please, can you help? My grandfather will be 85 in July. We don't have a lot of money, and we want to do something really special for him. He's very independent and has many interests, but we can't think what to do. Any suggestions?

He likes movies, but he doesn't like to go out to movie theaters, and his TV gets very bad reception. He really loves Italian food, but there aren't any good restaurants around here. He enjoys music, but his stereo doesn't always work very well. He's also interested in other countries, but he can't travel anymore. His house is big and hard to clean, but he won't move to a new one.

Arby, please give us some ideas.

CONFUSED Cleveland, Ohio

Dear Confused,

Your grandfather sounds like a very special person. Here are some ideas to help you. Why don't

you _____

_____

Here are some other things you can do: _____

_____

_____

You can also _____

_____

Good luck!

Arby

Activity 2

Congratulations! You've just won $100,000, but there is one condition: You have to spend one half of the money ($50,000) on your classmates.

Work with a partner to make a list here, giving the reason for each gift beside it.

When you are ready, tell the class what gifts you have decided on.

Gift	Person	Reason

Activity 3

A famous United States President, John F. Kennedy, once said, "Ask not what your country can do for you; ask what you can do for your country." Discuss the meaning of this statement.

(Kennedy used the more formal "Ask not" rather than "Do not ask" or "Don't ask." Why do you think this is so?)

Activity 4

Form a group of at least five people. It is lunchtime and you are very hungry. A member of your group has volunteered to go to the local fast-food restaurant to pick up a hamburger, a chicken sandwich, or a hot dog for you. Look at the menu below and decide on your order.

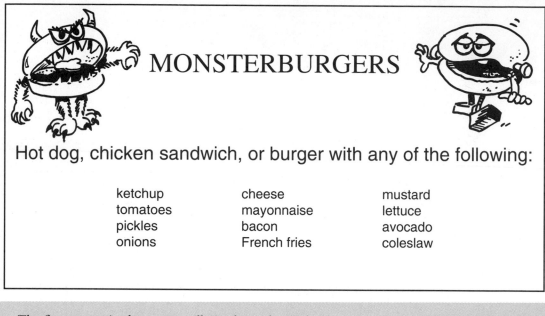

MONSTERBURGERS

Hot dog, chicken sandwich, or burger with any of the following:

ketchup	cheese	mustard
tomatoes	mayonnaise	lettuce
pickles	bacon	avocado
onions	French fries	coleslaw

The first person in the group will give his or her order:

Carmen: I'm ordering a hot dog with mustard and ketchup and French fries for me.

The second person repeats the last order and adds his or her own.

Lu: I'm ordering a hot dog with mustard and ketchup and French fries for Carmen and a chicken sandwich with lettuce, tomato, and avocado for me.

The third person repeats Carmen and Lu's orders and adds his or her own. Continue like this until you have remembered everybody's order.

Finally, try to do this with the whole class!

Activity 5

Work in a group.

Choose one of the verb and prepositions from the list below. Prepare to act out a skit or short situation that demonstrates the verb. You can speak, but **you must not use the verb itself**. Your classmates will try to guess the verb you chose.

Your teacher will demonstrate this for you first.

give to	buy for	carry to	carry for
open for	make for	cook for	knit for
fix for	hand to	send to	sell to

Now, choose one of the statements from the list below. With your group, prepare to act out a skit or short situation to demonstrate the statement, **but do not use the statement itself.** Your classmates will try to guess which one you chose. Your teacher will demonstrate this for you first.

He/She bought him/her (something).

He/She cooked him/her (something).

He/She made him/her (something).

He/She carried (something) for him/her.

He/She built (something) for someone.

He/She bought (something) for him/her.

He/She cooked (something) for him/her.

He/She made (something) for him/her.

He/She opened (something) for him/her.

He/She built him/her (something).

22

The Passive

Task

You are gathering information for a book on Campinilea, an island located off the coast of Peru. The first chapter of the book is called "The Products and Natural Resources of Campinilea." Use the map to match the resources with the places they are found:

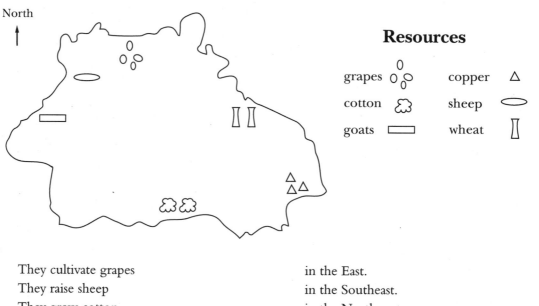

They cultivate grapes	in the East.
They raise sheep	in the Southeast.
They grow cotton	in the Northwest.
They grow wheat	in the North.
They mine copper	in the West.
They raise goats	in the South.

Which of the following statements sounds better for your chapter on the products and natural resources of Campinilea?

Grapes are cultivated in the North. OR **They cultivate grapes in the North.**

Why do you think this is so?

Focus 1

USE
Passive versus Active

USE

- The active voice emphasizes *the person* who performs an action:

  (a) Farmers cultivate grapes in the North.
- When you want to emphasize *the action or result of the action* and not the person who performs it, you can use the passive:

  (b) Grapes are cultivated in the North.
- We often use the passive when we do not know exactly who performed an action or when it is not important to know who performed it.
- The passive is more formal than the active and is therefore more common in writing, particularly scientific and technological writing, than in conversation. The passive is also very common in news reports.

Focus 2

FORM
How to Form the Passive

FORM

- To form the passive, use the appropriate tense of *be*, followed by the past participle (pp):

Simple Present	am/is/are	+ pp	Beer **is produced** here.
Present Progressive	am/is/are being	+ pp	Beer **is being produced** here right now.
Simple Past	was/were	+ pp	Beer **was produced** here.
Past Progressive	was/were being	+ pp	Beer **was being produced** here ten years ago.
Present Perfect	have/has been	+ pp	Beer **has been produced** here since 1900.
Past Perfect	had been	+ pp	Beer **had been produced** here when the island was discovered.
Future (will)	will be	+ pp	Beer **will be produced** here next year.
Future (be going to)	am/is/are going to be	+ pp	Beer **is going to be produced** here.

- Present perfect progressive and past perfect progressive are rarely used in the passive.

Exercise 1

Change the statements about the natural resources of Campinilea in the Task so that they more appropriately fit a chapter on the topic of products and natural resources. The first one has been done for you.

1. *Grapes are cultivated in the North* _____ .

2. _____ .

3. _____ .

4. _____ .

5. _____ .

6. _____ .

Exercise 2

The second chapter of the book on Campinilea is called "The People of Campinilea and their Customs." Look at the following statements about Campinilea; write *1* beside those which you think belong to Chapter 1 (Products and Resources) and *2* beside those which you think belong to Chapter 2 (People and Customs).

1. In the West, unmarried women leave their family homes at the age of 25 and raise goats in the mountains.
2. Miners mined silver throughout the island during the last century.
3. They will plant the first crop of rice in the South next year.
4. In the Southeast, fathers take their oldest sons to the copper mines on their 12th birthday in a special ceremony to teach them the legends and rituals associated with Campinilean copper.
5. Easterners are more traditional than Southerners; for example, farmers in the East have harvested wheat in the same way for hundreds of years, while those in the South are constantly exploring new techniques for growing cotton.
6. They have produced grapes in Campinilea for only a few years.

Do you think it would be appropriate to use the passive in any of these statements? Why do you think this? Rewrite those statements here:

_____

_____

_____

Exercise 3

Complete the following report about the products of Campinilea, using the appropriate form of the passive.

Campinilea is well-known for a number of products that are popular with tourists. For example, traditional sweaters (1) _are made_ (make) from the wool that (2) _is produced_ (produce) in the Northwest. This wool (3) _is_ also _sent_ (send) to the Southwest region of the island, where it (4) _is woven_ (weave) into colorful rugs. These rugs (5) _are sold_ (sell) all over the world. Another popular product is jewelry. Rings and necklaces in traditional designs (6) _are made_ (make) from the copper that (7) _is mined_ (mine) in the Southeast. The wine that (8) _is served_ (serve) in restaurants in the capital (9) _is made_ (make) from grapes that (10) _are cultivated_ (cultivate) in the North. Visitors also enjoy Campinilean cheeses and bread, all of which (11) _are produced_ (produce) locally.

Exercise 4

Complete the following, using appropriate tenses.

Adventurous tourists are beginning to discover Campinilea, and the island is hard at work getting ready to welcome more visitors. A new airport (1) _was built_ (build) last year, and at the moment, hotels (2) _are being constructed_ (construct) along the southern beaches. A new road (3) _will be finished_ (finish) next year so visitors will be able to reach the northern region. Five years ago, very little (4) _was known_ (know) about Campinilea; but last year, three books (5) _were written_ (write) about the island, and several guide books (6) _were published_ (publish). At the moment, these books (7) _are being translated_ (translate) into different languages. English (8) _is taught_ (teach) in schools so many Campinileans know a little English, but not many other foreign languages (9) _is spoken_ (speak).

Tourism has brought many changes to this small island, and people are afraid that it will have a negative effect on the traditional customs and culture of the people. For example, last month in the capital, several young Campinileans (10) _were arrested_ (arrest) for being drunk in public, and some tourists (11) _were robbed_ (rob) near the beach. However, if you leave the tourist areas and go up to the mountains, you will find that life is still the same as it was hundreds of years ago. For example, since the sixteenth century, the same tribal dances (12) _have been performed_ (perform) to celebrate the Campinilean new year, and the same type of food (13) _has been served_ (serve). For centuries, visitors (14) _have been invited_ (invite) to join Campinileans in the celebration of festivals, and you will find traditional Campinilean hospitality in these regions has not changed at all.

Focus 3

USE

Including the Agent

USE

- We can include the agent (the person who performs an action) in the passive in the following situations:
  - To add new information:
    - **(a)** Tribal dances are performed every night. During the week, they are performed **by women**, and on weekends they are performed **by men**.

    In this case, it is necessary to include the agents *by women* and *by men* because they add **new** information to our knowledge of tribal dances.

    Compare these two statements:
    - **(b)** Wheat is grown in the East.
    - **(c)** Wheat is grown in the East by farmers.

    Sentence (c) sounds strange because **we already know** or **understand** the identity of the agent (farmers) from the context. Therefore, when you know or understand the identity of the agent, the *by* + agent phrase is unnecessary.

- With proper names or well-known people:

  (d) Campinilea was discovered by Francisco Pizarro.

  The agent is important here because Pizarro is well known. The *by* + agent phrase is commonly used to talk about works of art, well-known inventions, discoveries, historical events, and famous achievements:

  (e) *Hamlet* was written **by William Shakespeare**.

  (f) Many South American countries were liberated **by Simón Bolivar**.

- When the identity of the agent is unexpected or surprising:

  (g) I can't believe it! This novel was written by **a fourteen-year-old**.

- It is important to keep in mind, however, that in most of the situations where the passive is used, the *by* + agent phrase does not occur.

Exercise 5

Decide if the *by* + agent phrase is necessary in all of the following. Cross out the *by* phrases that you think are unnecessary.

1. Copper has been mined by miners for hundreds of years in Campinilea.
2. Campinilea was described by Jules Verne in one of his novels. ✓
3. Cotton is grown by Campinileans in the south of Campinilea.
4. Hotels are being built by builders along the southern beaches.
5. Campinilea was colonized by the Spanish for many years. ✓
6. English is taught by teachers in Campinilean schools.
7. Wheat is grown by Campinileans in eastern Campinilea. It is planted by men, and it is harvested by women and children. ✓
8. Next year several new hotels in Campinilia will be built by American developers. ✓
9. Rugs have been produced by people in Campinilea for centuries. They are woven by women from the mountain tribes and are then transported to the capital by mule and are sold in the markets by relatives of the weavers. ✓
10. In restaurants in the city, fine Campinilean wines are served by waiters. These wines are rarely drunk by Campinileans, but they are much appreciated by foreign tourists. ✓

Exercise 6

With the growth of tourism, petty crime has unfortunately increased in Campinilea. The Campinilean police are currently investigating a robbery that took place in a hotel room a few nights ago.

Work with a partner. One of you should look at page 245 (Picture A), and one of you should look at page 247 (Picture B). One of you has a picture of the room **before** the robbery, and the other has a picture of the room **after** the robbery. Seven different things were done to the room. *Without looking at your partner's picture*, find what these seven things were and complete the report below.

Last night the police were called in to investigate a robbery that took place at the Hotel Paraiso. The identity of the thief is still unknown. The police took note of several unusual occurrences. For

example _____

_____

_____

Members of the public have been asked to contact the police with any information about the identity of the thief. Any information leading to an arrest will be rewarded.

Activities

Activity 1

Work in pairs. Try to think of 20 different achievements (discoveries, inventions, or works of art), as well as the name of the person(s) who created them. For example:

The telephone   Alexander Graham Bell

(There are some more ideas to get you going at the bottom of the page, but you probably have better ideas of your own.)

Write each name on an index card and then write each achievement on a *different* index card. You should have a total of 40 cards:

Hamlet

William Shakespeare

Now you are ready to play Achievement Snap:

1. Get together with another pair. Put all your "People Cards" in one deck and all your "Achievement Cards" in another deck. Shuffle each deck carefully.

2. Put the deck of Achievement Cards facedown on a table.

3. Deal the People Cards to the players. Each player should have several cards. Do not look at your cards.

4. The dealer turns over the first Achievement Card and puts down his/her first People Card. The object of the game is to make a correct match between Achievement and Person.

5. Keep taking turns at putting down People Cards until a match is made. The first person to spot a match shouts "snap" loudly and verbalizes the match: "The telephone was invented by Alexander Graham Bell." If everyone agrees that the match is factually correct **and** grammatical, the player takes the pile of People Cards on the table.

6. The winner is the person who collects the most People Cards.

(Note: It is still possible to continue playing after you lose all your People Cards. If you correctly spot a "match," you can collect the cards on the table.)

Some ideas:

Mona Lisa	Leonardo da Vinci
hydrogen bomb	Edward Teller
photography	Louis Daguerre
War and Peace	Leo Tolstoy
"Yesterday"	John Lennon and Paul McCartney
Psycho	Alfred Hitchcock
Mount Everest	Tenzing

Remember to use an appropriate verb in matching the person and the achievement. Common verbs include: *compose, write, discover, invent, climb, direct, sing, paint.*

PICTURE A

Activity 2

Make a presentation (oral or written) on your country or on a place that you know well. Describe the resources and products, any changes over time, and any predictions for the future.

Activity 3

It has been suggested that young people today do not have enough "general knowledge" and that they know less about the world than older people do. The purpose of this activity is to make a survey of your local community to find out if this is true. You will be interviewing North Americans of different ages and finding out about their levels of knowledge on a number of general topics.

The categories of the survey are as follows:

Discoveries   Inventions   Works of art

First, form specific project groups. One group will survey knowledge of discoveries, another, knowledge of inventions, and another, knowledge of works of art. In your group, decide on ten questions on your topic. For example, under the topic of discoveries, you could include:

Who was Brazil discovered by?

Who was radium discovered by?

You may need to research your topics in a library to be sure of your own answers. Next, share your group's proposed questions with the rest of the class to see what feedback and suggestions they give you. Decide on how many people you should all survey.

After that, administer your survey by asking native speakers the questions and noting their answers. You should also take note of their gender, their occupations, and their age category; for example, under 18 / 18 – 25 / 26 – 35 / 36 – 45 / 46 – 55 / over 55. (You need to be careful with this, because many people are sensitive about their ages.) Each person in the group is responsible for interviewing a specific number of different people.

When you have gathered all your information, meet with your group to share your findings. Put all your group's data together and decide how best to present your results. Use charts and diagrams as necessary. Present your group's findings to the rest of the class.

Finally, write a report of the results of the whole survey, showing the general conclusions. Remember to announce your purpose in writing the report; for example:

It has been argued that young people today do not have enough general knowledge and that they know less about the world than older people do. Our class was interested in finding out if this was true for people in our local community. In this report, I will describe the survey we designed and discuss the results we obtained.

Activity 4

Walk around your neighborhood or city. What is being done to make it a better place to live in?

Report on your findings to your classmates: While I was walking in the neighborhood, I noticed that. . . .

In what ways do you think your neighborhood/city will be a better place in the future?

PICTURE B

23

Get-Passive

Task

What do you think probably happened?

explain pictures

Now match the captions to the pictures.

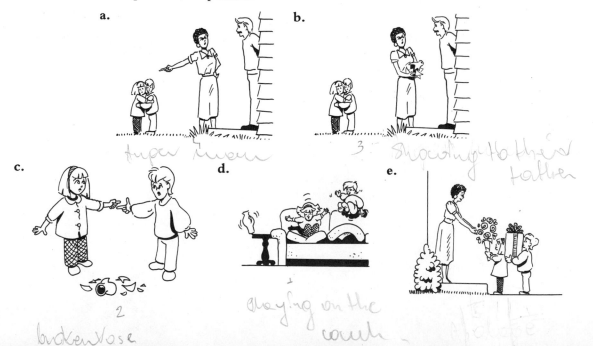

a.

b.

tiger man   *3 shouting to their father*

c.

d.

e.

broken nose   *2*   *playing on the couch*

1. **A:** It's **your** fault. You broke it!   _____
   B: No I didn't! **You** did it!
2. Your children broke my vase.   _____
3. We're very sorry that we broke your vase.   _____
4. This vase was broken by your children!   _____
5. It was an accident! We were playing on the couch, and, somehow the vase got broken.   _____

Focus 1

USE

Be-Passive versus *Get*-Passive

USE

- Unit 22 discusses the way you can emphasize an action or result over its agent by using the passive (*be* + past participle). Another way to do this is to use the *get*-passive:

  (a) Her car was stolen last night.

  (b) Her car got stolen last night.

- We usually use the *get*-passive to talk about unexpected actions or events—things which happen suddenly and without warning:

  (c) It suddenly started to rain and we all got soaked.

  (d) She got hit by a car while she was crossing the road.

Exercise 1

Look back at the statements in the Task. Why do you think the passive is used in some of these statements and not in others? Why do you think the *get*-passive is used in 5?

Focus 2

When to Use *Get*-Passive

USE

- *Get*-passives are more informal than passives with *be*. *Get*-passives are very common in conversation but are usually not appropriate in writing or in more formal spoken situations:
  - **(a)** To a friend: Have you heard the news? Isao's car **got stolen**!
  - **(b)** From a police report: A white Honda Civic **was stolen** last night.
- The agent + *by* phrase are not usually included in *get*-passive statements.

Exercise 2

Read the following situations. What do you think probably happened before each one? Match the situation with one of the previous events in the box below.

SITUATION	PREVIOUS EVENT
1. Oh, no! Not my clean white shirt!	b
2. We're finally able to pay our bills.	f
3. It's so exciting to see my name in print.	g
4. I told you not to leave it outside at night!	h
5. When I came back to the parking lot, I found these dents on the side.	b
6. They took him straight to the hospital by ambulance.	c
7. Thank you for all your support. Now that I am mayor, I will work to improve our schools.	a
8. The packet's empty, and there are only a few crumbs left!	e

---

(a) They got paid.

(b) His car got hit.

(c) Someone got injured.

(d) Some wine got spilled.

(e) All the cookies got eaten.

(f) She got elected to public office.

(g) His book got published.

(h) Her bike got stolen.

250

Focus 3

FORM

How to Form the *Get*-Passive

FORM

- We can use the *get*-passive with a variety of tenses. (pp = past participle)

Present Simple	get	+	pp	Her cookies always **get eaten**.
Present Progressive	am/is/are getting	+	pp	Her cookies **are getting eaten**.
Past Simple	got	+	pp	Her cookies **got eaten**.
Past Progressive	was/were getting	+	pp	Her cookies **were getting eaten**.
Present Perfect	have/has gotten	+	pp	Her cookies **have gotten eaten**.
Past Perfect	had gotten	+	pp	Her cookies **had gotten eaten**.
Future (will)	will get	+	pp	Her cookies **will get eaten**.
(going to)	am/is/are going to get	+	pp	Her cookies are **going to get eaten**.

- QUESTIONS: Simple present and past:

Do/does +	subject +	*get* +	pp	Do her cookies **get eaten**?
Did +	subject +	*get* +	pp	Did her cookies **get eaten**?

- NEGATIVE: Simple present and past:

subject +	*do/does* + (*don't/doesn't*)	*not* +	*get* +	pp	Her cookies **do not get eaten**.
subject +	*did* + (*didn't*)	*not* +	*get* +	pp	Her cookies **did not get eaten**.

Exercise 3

Complete the following with *get*-passive and the appropriate tense.

1. **A:** I think I've prepared too much food for tomorrow's party.

   B: Don't worry. It _____ all _____ (eat).

2. **A:** Where's your car?

   B: It's _____ (fix).

251

3. **A:** How was your vacation last month?

   B: Terrible. We _____ (rob) and all our traveler's checks _____ (take).

4. **A:** Have you heard? Chuck _____ (invite) to dinner with the President at the White House!

   B: I don't believe it.

5. **A:** Please drive more slowly.

   B: Why?

   A: If you don't, we _____ (stop) by the Highway Patrol.

6. **A:** Are your assignments ready yet?

   B: Almost. We finished writing them last night, and now they _____ (type).

7. **A:** Do you know if Sid has moved?

   B: No. Why?

   A: I sent him a letter last week, but it _____ (return) yesterday with no forwarding address.

   B: That's strange.

8. **A:** Al's writing a novel.

   B: Really?

   A: Yes. He hopes it _____ (publish) next year.

9. **A:** Rosa quit her job.

   B: Why?

   A: She _____ (not/pay).

10. **A:** There was a terrible accident here last night.

    B: _____ anyone _____ (hurt)?

Focus 4

Using *Get*-Passive to Show Change

USE

- The *get*-passive emphasizes a **change** in a situation:

(a)	We were soaked to the skin.	(Emphasis on the result of the rain.)
(b)	We got soaked to the skin.	(Emphasis on the process of becoming wet in the rain.)
(c)	He was injured in a car crash.	(Emphasis on the result of the car crash.)
(d)	He got injured in a car crash.	(Emphasis on the **change**: He wasn't injured before, but now he is.)

- The *get*-passive is therefore used with verbs that express actions and processes, not with existing "states":

  (e) The answer was known. (**Known** = existing state.)
  NOT: The answer got known.

  (f) They are married. (Emphasis on existing state.)

  (g) They got married last year. (Emphasis on the change in their marital status.)

SOME COMMON STATIVE VERBS

We do not generally use these verbs with *get*-passive:

own	*see*	*understand*
like	*love*	*feel*
hate	*know*	*want*

- See Unit 2 for more information on stative verbs.

Exercise 4

Where possible, rewrite the underlined verbs with *get*-passives.

1. Last week, Mervin had a dinner party. He prepared lots of food, and everything <u>was eaten</u>. ___

   _____

2. This ring is very valuable because it <u>was owned</u> by Napoleon. _____

   _____

3. We are very sorry that Mr. Gordon is leaving our company—he <u>was liked</u> and respected by us all. _____

4. What happened to your car?

   It <u>was hit</u> by a truck. _____

5. Someone broke into her house, but surprisingly, nothing <u>was taken</u>. _____

   _____

6. At the time of his arrest, that man was armed and dangerous, and he <u>was wanted</u> by police in three different states. _____

7. We really hope our book <u>will be published</u> some day. _____

   _____

8. I'm sorry I'm late; I had to go to the veterinarian's because my dog <u>was attacked</u> by a cat. _____

   _____

9. Many beautiful houses <u>were</u> badly <u>damaged</u> in last month's earthquake. _____

   _____

10. Marilyn Monroe <u>was loved</u> by many famous men. _____

    _____

Exercise 5

Tabloid newspapers present sensational, but usually untrue, stories. Look at the following tabloid newspaper headlines and rewrite each one as a complete sentence. Use a *get*-passive wherever possible; use a *be*-passive where you cannot use a *get*-passive.

1. BABY KILLED BY GIANT COCKROACHES
2. ELVIS SEEN IN SUPERMARKET LINE
3. VICE-PRESIDENT KIDNAPPED BY SPACE ALIENS
4. BILL AND HILLARY TO DIVORCE?
5. WORLD'S WORST HUSBAND MARRIED 36 TIMES
6. FALSE TEETH STUCK IN MAN'S THROAT FOR SIX MONTHS

   What do you think each headline is about? Why?

Activities

Activity 1

Look at the following tabloid headlines and ask a native speaker to explain what she or he thinks the headline means. Tape the conversation and then listen to the recording to see if she or he uses any passive forms in his or her explanation. Share your findings with the rest of the class.

WOMAN HYPNOTIZED BY ALIENS

MAN'S LIFE SAVED BY HITCHHIKING GHOST

SUITCASE DROPPED 5,000 FEET BY AIRLINE

HUBBY BURNS TO A CRISP AS WOODEN LEG TORCHED BY WIFE

WOMAN PREGNANT WITH DAUGHTER'S BABY

Activity 2

In this activity, you will make a chain story about somebody's bad day—a day when everything went wrong. One student will start the story and will continue until she or he uses a *get*-passive. When she or he uses a *get*-passive, the next person will continue.

Student 1: Andy had a really bad day. First, he overslept. When he got dressed, he forget to put his pants on.

Student 2: He ran out of the house, but he got embarrassed when he realized he had forgotten his pants.

Student 3: etc., etc.

Activity 3

Have **you** ever had a really bad day? A day when everything went wrong, through no fault of your own? Describe the day, using *get*-passive where possible.

Activity 4

The purpose of this activity is to analyze native speakers' use of *get*-passives. Arrange to have a conversation with a native-speaker of English. Ask him or her to tell you about a really frightening experience s/he once had. Find out how it happened. Tape your conversation, and afterward listen to your recording to see if the *get*-passive was used and in what ways. Share your findings with the rest of the class.

Modals of Probability and Possibility

Could, May, Might, Must

Task

One evening toward the end of March, a New York taxi driver found that someone had left a briefcase on the back seat of his cab. When he opened it, he found that the briefcase was empty, except for the things you can see on pages 257 and 258. Examine these carefully. Can you find any clues about the identity of the owner of the briefcase? Use the chart below to write down your ideas and to show how certain you are about them.

GUESSES	HOW CERTAIN ARE YOU?		
	Less Than 50% Certain (it's possible)	**90% Certain (it's probable)**	**100% Certain (it's certain)**
Name			
Sex			
Age			
Marital Status			
Occupation			
Likes and Interests			
Family and Friends			
Habits			
Recent Activities			
Future Plans			
Anything else?			

SUNDAY	MONDAY	TUESDAY	WEDNESDAY	THURSDAY	FRIDAY	SATURDAY	**MAR**
1	2 *Board meeting 10:30* *Send papers to Washington*	3 *meeting 8* *lunch: Sally* *1.* *leave for NYC: 7:00*	4 Ash Wednesday *NYC EXECUTIVE*	5 *MEETING*	6 *Return from NYC meeting: 10:30* *drinks: Bob Theater 8:30*	7 *wedding anniversary* *dinner - 8*	
8 *golf 9:30*	9 *Report on NYC meeting due*	10 *Sally's birthday meeting with vice president 2 p.m. movie 8*	11 *PARIS* *arrive: 14.50*	12 *MEETING*	13	14 *Call Sally*	
15 Purim	16 *Accountant: 9 lunch: Robert Hayward Call Paris office*	17 St. Patrick's Day *Opera 7:30*	18 *Visitors from Tokyo office dinner: Japanese restaurant - 7 p.m.*	19	20 *Export meeting*	21 Spring Begins *tennis 2 p.m. Mike* *kids home from school*	
22 *golf 9:30*	23 *Japanese class*	24 *doctor: 8 Sales meeting 10:30*	25 *9:00 accountant tennis: Mike*	26 *lunch: Sally*	27 *doctor: 9 10:00 sales meeting Japanese class*	28 *check passport*	
29 *TOKYO?*	30	31					

Focus 1

Expressing Possibility and Probability

USE

• There are several ways of expressing possibility or probability. The form you choose depends on how certain you feel about the topic:

	Possible (less than 50% certain)	Probable (about 90% certain)	Certain (100% certain)
More Certain ↑ ↓ **Less Certain**	**(a)** He *may* smoke. **(b)** He *might* smoke. **(c)** He *could* smoke.	**(g)** He *must* smoke.	**(i)** He *smokes*.
More Certain ↑ ↓ **Less Certain**	**(d)** She *may* be a doctor. **(e)** She *might* be a doctor. **(f)** She *could* be a doctor.	**(h)** She *must* be a doctor.	**(j)** She *is* a doctor.

• For information on some other ways of using *could, might, may* and *must*, see Units 7, 8, and 15.

Focus 2

Modals of Probability and Possibility

FORM

- *Could, might, may* and *must* are modal auxiliaries, and like most other modal auxiliaries, they are followed by the infinitive without *to*:
  - **(a)** That woman looks familiar: She **could be** a movie star.
  - **(b)** Lila always gets excellent grades: She **must study** a lot.
- They do not change to agree with the subject:

(c) You **must know** a lot of interesting people.	Carol **must know** a lot of interesting people.
(d) They **might be** janitors, but I doubt it.	He **might be** a janitor, but I doubt it.
(e) I **may have** the information you need.	Shirley **may have** the information you need.

- Negatives are formed without *do*:

(f) She **must not** like cats.	They **might not** know about the party.

Exercise 1

Turn back to the Task.

Make statements about the owner of the briefcase. Use *could, might, may,* or *must* to show how certain you feel. Share your opinions with your classmates and be ready to justify them as necessary.

EXAMPLE: NAME: *In my opinion, the owner of the briefcase might be called C. Murray because this name is on the boarding pass. However, this boarding pass could belong to somebody else.*

1. SEX: In my opinion, the owner of the briefcase _____

   because _____

   _____ .

2. OCCUPATION: I believe she or he _____ because _____

   _____ .

3. MARITAL STATUS: This person _____ . I think this because

   _____ .

4. LIKES AND INTERESTS: _____

_____

5. HABITS: _____

_____

6. AGE: _____

_____

Focus 3

FORM

Probability and Possibility in the Past

FORM

- To express possibility and probability in the past:
  - Modal auxiliary + *have* + past participle
    - **(a)** I'm not sure how Liz went home; she **could have taken** a cab.
    - **(b)** There's nobody here; they **must have gone** out.

Exercise 2

Turn back to the Task. Make statements showing how certain you are about the person's **past** activities. Use *could, might, may,* or *must* as appropriate. Be ready to share and justify your opinions.

Exercise 3

In trying to solve crimes, detectives generally examine evidence carefully and then draw conclusions based on what they observe. Sometimes their conclusions are stronger (or more certain) than others, depending on the evidence they have examined. Creative detectives (like Sherlock Holmes) are famous for examining *all* possibilities in a case. What might Sherlock Holmes conclude about the following people?

> **EXAMPLE:** 1. A woman with a yellow forefinger: *She must be a heavy smoker.*
> *She might be a painter, and she might have lost her paintbrush.*

Can you think of any other possibilities? Be ready to share your ideas with your classmates.

2. A very short man with bow legs: _____

_____

_____

3. A man with a very red nose: _____

_____

_____

4. A woman with rough, hard hands: _____

_____

_____

5. A woman with a fur coat, diamonds, and chauffeur-driven limousine: _____

_____

_____

6. A man with soft, white hands: _____

_____

_____

7. A man with a lot of tattoos: _____

_____

_____

Exercise 4

The police are investigating a murder. What might Sherlock Holmes conclude about the following pieces of evidence? Get together with your classmates to share your conclusions and decide who has the most interesting theory. How probable do you think this theory is?

> The victim was found in her bedroom on the second floor of her house. The front door and her bedroom door were locked from inside. There were two wine glasses on the table in her room; one was empty, the other was full. There was an ashtray with several cigarette butts in it. The victim had a small white button in her hand and several long, blond hairs. Her watch was found on the floor; it had stopped at 11:30. The drawers of the victim's desk were open, and there were papers all over the floor. Nothing appeared to be missing.

Exercise 5

You are a reporter for your local newspaper. The editor has asked you to report on the murder described in Exercise 4, describing what you think happened and why you believe this to be so. Make a headline for your report. Display your headline and your report so that your classmates can compare the different theories about the murder.

Focus 4

FORM ● MEANING

Future Probability and Possibility

FORM
MEANING

- *Could, might,* and *may* all express possibility in the future:

    (a) There are a few clouds in the sky; it $\left\{ \begin{array}{l} \textbf{could} \\ \textbf{might} \\ \textbf{may} \end{array} \right\}$ rain later.

    May shows that the speaker is a little more certain.

- *Must* is not used to express probability in the future. Instead, *will* and *be going to + probably* usually express this idea:

    (b) A: Where's Anna?
        B: She'll probably get here soon.

    (c) A: What's Jim going to do after he graduates?
        B: He's probably going to travel round the world on a motorcycle.

- We use *will* and *be going to* to express certainty about the future. For more information on how to use *be going to* and *will*, see Unit 3.

Exercise 6

Turn back to the Task. From the evidence given, what can you say about the person's **future** plans? Use *could, might, may, be going to,* or *will* + *probably* as necessary. Be prepared to share and justify your answers.

Exercise 7

Choose the *best* form from the choices given below.

1. **A:** Where's Rose?
   B: I'm not sure. She _____ in the library.
   is   might be   must be

2. **A:** My daughter just got a scholarship to Stanford!
   B: You _____ be very proud of her.
   could   must   might

3. **A:** How does Sheila get to school?
   B: I don't really know. She _____ the bus.
   might take   takes   must take

4. **A:** It's really cold in here today.
   B: Yes. Somebody _____ the window open.
   must leave   might leave   must have left

5. **A:** I wonder why Zelda always wears gloves.
   B: I don't know. She _____ some kind of allergy.
   may have had   has   may have

6. **A:** Have you heard the weather forecast?
   B: No, but look at all those dark clouds in the sky. I think it _____ rain.
   could   must   is probably going to

7. **A:** Did my mother call while I was out?
   B: I'm not sure. She _____ .
   might have   might   did

8. **A:** Ellen gave a violin recital in front of 500 people yesterday. It was her first public performance.
   B: Really? She _____ very nervous.
   could have been   must be   must have been

9. **A:** Are you coming to Jeff's party?
   B: I'm not sure. I _____ go to the coast instead.
   must   will   might

10. **A:** Can I speak to Professor Carroll?
    B: She's not in her office, and she doesn't have any more classes today, so she _____ home.
    might go   must have gone   will probably go

Exercise 8

Look back at the Task. Who is this person? What do you think happened to him or her? Complete the following newspaper article with your ideas about what might have happened to him or her.

MISSING MYSTERY PERSON

It has been a week since New York taxi driver Ricardo Oliveiro found a briefcase on the back seat of his cab. It has been a week of guessing and speculation: Who is the owner of this briefcase and where is he or she now? Several different theories have been proposed, but so far the most interesting is the one which follows....

Activities

Activity 1

Can you guess what these drawings represent? Get together with a partner and see how many *different* possible interpretations you can come up with for each drawing. Classify your interpretations as "Possible," "Probable," and "Certain." Compare your answers with the rest of the class. (You can find the "official" answers on page 267.)

The purpose of this activity is to confuse your classmates. Form teams and create five different drawings of familiar things seen from an unusual point of view. Exchange papers. Each team receives drawings from another team. As a team, see how many different interpretations you can make for each drawing. Write them beside the drawing, showing how probable you think your interpretation is.

EXAMPLE:

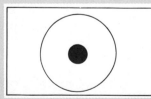

It could be a donut.
It might be a hat from above.
It could be an eyeball.

When you have made your guesses, exchange papers with another team until everyone has had a chance to "interpret" all the drawings. Which team got the most "correct" interpretations? Which team had the most creative interpretations?

Activity 2

Get together with a partner and examine the photographs below. What's going on? Who are the people? Create a story showing what you think might have happened and what might happen next. You can use the photographs in any order that you like. Compare your story with those of your classmates. In what ways do their interpretations differ from yours?

Activity 3

Show the photographs from Activity 2 to a native speaker. Ask him or her to tell you what she or he thinks might have happened and what might happen next. If possible, tape the answers. Listen to the tape and take special note of the different ways the native speaker expresses possibility and probability. Share your findings with the rest of the class.

Activity 4

In the Task, you looked at the contents of somebody's briefcase and made guesses about his or her identity. The purpose of this activity is to create your own "mystery person." Form groups and collect a number of items that somebody might carry in his/her pockets (tickets, bills, photographs, business cards, etc.). Choose between eight to ten items, put them in a bag, and bring them to class. Exchange bags with another group. With your group, examine the contents of your bag and try to decide on the possible identity of the owner, using the same categories as the Task. When everyone is ready, share your conclusions with the rest of the class, showing how certain you are. Remember, your classmates might ask you to justify your conclusions, so be ready to justify each one.

Activity 5

Write a profile of the mystery person your group presented to the class in Activity 4. Make sure you have an introduction and that you provide evidence to support your conclusions. When you finish writing, read your profile to see how much of the language discussed in this unit you were able to use.

"Official" Answers to Activity 1

1. A giraffe passing a window.
2. A pencil seen from the end.
3. A cat climbing a tree.

Noun Complements

That Clauses

Task

A. React to each of the following statements, using the following scale:

1	2	3	4	5
strongly agree	agree	neutral/ no opinion	disagree	strongly disagree

In the next ten years . . .

1. we will find a cure for AIDS.   1 2 3 4 5
2. the rain forests will disappear.   1 2 3 4 5
3. marijuana will be legalized in western countries.   1 2 3 4 5
4. people will become less dependent on automobiles.   1 2 3 4 5
5. crime will decrease.   1 2 3 4 5
6. we will stop killing animals for their fur.   1 2 3 4 5
7. homelessness will decrease.   1 2 3 4 5
8. communism as a political system will disappear entirely.   1 2 3 4 5
9. women will have the same economic rights as men.   1 2 3 4 5
10. there will be less racial discrimination.   1 2 3 4 5
11. there will be another world war.   1 2 3 4 5
12. drinking, like smoking, will become socially less acceptable.   1 2 3 4 5

B. Now find out what other students have said and tell them your opinions, using:

"I agree/strongly agree with the statement that in ten years . . ."
OR "I disagree/strongly disagree with the statement that in ten years . . ."
OR "I am neutral or have no opinion about the statement that in ten years . . ."

C. Report your class's opinions by using "think that," "believe that," "feel that," etc. For example, "Five people believe that . . . ," "Three people don't think that . . ."

Focus 1

FORM ● MEANING

Using *That* Clauses in Sentences

FORM
MEANING

- We often use *that* clauses (the word *that* + a sentence) with verbs that express beliefs, ideas, opinions, or facts.

    I know that. . . .
    I believe that. . . .
    I think that. . . .
    I doubt that. . . .

- A *that* clause is a noun phrase. It can be used as an object to complete a sentence.

Subject	Verb	Direct Object
The police	think	that they know who robbed the bank.

Exercise 1

What do you think about some of the statements in the Task? Complete the following to make statements that are true for you.

1. I know that
2. I am not certain that
3. I am convinced that
4. I doubt that

5. It is my opinion that
6. It is unlikely that
7. It is possible that
8. It is doubtful that

Focus 2

Making *That* Clauses Negative

FORM
MEANING

- To make a sentence with a *that* clause negative, the word *not* usually comes in the first part of the sentence—in the main clause, not in the *that* clause.

Main Clause	*That* Clause
(a) I **don't** think	that we will stop killing animals for fur.
NOT: I think	that we will **not** stop killing animals for fur.

- You can also make a *that* clause negative by using words which already include a "negative" meaning, such as *doubt, unlikely, uncertain.*
  (b) I **doubt** that we will stop killing animals for fur.
  (c) It is **unlikely** that we will stop killing animals for fur.

Exercise 2

Did you disagree with some of the opinions expressed in the Task? Tell some of your "negative" reactions, using *not* in your statement, and say why your opinion differs.

EXAMPLE: *I don't believe that there will be another World War in the next ten years because. . . .*

Focus 3

USE

When to Omit the Word *That*

USE

- With verbs like *know, believe,* and *think,* we can omit the word *that,* especially in speech, when it's not necessary to be formal.
  (a) Informal: I know the Taj Mahal's in India.
  (b) More formal: I know that the Taj Mahal is in India.

Exercise 3

Combine the two short statements in the conversation below into one longer statement using a *that* clause in your answer. If Person (b) starts his or her short statement with *It* or *That*, use *It* as the subject in your longer statement. (See Example 1.) If Person (b) starts his or her short statement with *I*, use that person's name as the subject in your longer statement. (See Example 2.)

> EXAMPLES: 1. **(a)** Betty: We can buy a car.
> **(b)** Bob: It's possible.
> *It's possible that Betty and Bob can buy a car.*
> 2. **(a)** Betty: It's raining.
> **(b)** Bob: I know.
> *Bob knows that it's raining.*

3. **(a)** Betty: My umbrella's broken.
   (b) Bob: That's unfortunate.

4. **(a)** Betty: We'll buy a car this week!
   (b) Bob: It's unlikely.

5. **(a)** Betty: I don't like my job.
   (b) Bob: That's too bad.

6. **(a)** Bob: I like my job.
   (b) Betty: I know.

7. **(a)** Bob: You should quit your job.
   (b) Betty: That's your opinion.

8. **(a)** Betty: We need the money.
   (b) Bob: I agree.

9. **(a)** Betty: The cost of living is rising.
   (b) Bob: It's true.

10. **(a)** Betty: I'm pregnant.
    (b) Bob: That's a surprise!

11. **(a)** Betty: We love each other.
    (b) Bob: We're lucky.

Exercise 4

Rewrite the following statements into one sentence, using a *that* clause. You do not need to use every word in the original statements as long as your statement makes sense and has all the important information.

> EXAMPLE: 1. Learning another language is important for everyone. This is what our English instructor thinks.
> *Our English instructor thinks (that) learning another language is important for everyone.*

2. An open-minded attitude is helpful in learning a language. This is what our English instructor believes.

3. Many Americans have never studied a foreign language. It is shocking.

4. Since English is an important world language used in business, it is not necessary to learn another language. This is what many Americans feel.

5. Learning another language is one way of showing respect to people from other countries. I believe this.

6. Some of us speak three or four languages. This amazes our English instructor.

Activities

Activity 1

Use the rating scale and the statements in the Task to interview native speakers of English for their opinions. Summarize the results of your survey for the rest of the class.

Activity 2

In teams, imagine that you are members of a group of "world citizens" who have been asked by a panel of international policy-makers to think about ways to solve one of the world's problems.

First, you will need to choose a world problem and discuss some of the steps that must be taken in order to begin solving this problem. Then you will need to make formal suggestions to the panel. Use the following sentence beginnings to guide you in making your report:

> We recommend that . . .
> We suggest that . . .
> We propose that . . .

Activity 3

In order to support your choices in Activity 2, you will need to make predictions about what might happen if your plan is *not* implemented/listened to. Use adjectives from the following list to make predictions about what could happen. (It is *certain* that . . . = strong prediction; It is *unlikely* that . . . = weak prediction.)

likely	unlikely
possible	certain
probable	doubtful

Activity 4

Before you present a final report to the international policymakers, you want to check to see if there is public support for your opinion. Make a short survey of people outside of your class to see if they agree with your opinions. You can model your survey after the Task, or you can design your own questionnaire, with a few specific questions about the issue you have chosen.

Activity 5

To follow up your work in the previous activities, write a short report that summarizes what you learned about one of the world's problems. In this report: 1) describe the problem; 2) report the results of the survey; 3) give your group's recommendations, and 4) predict the outcome if these recommendations are not followed.

26

Phrasal Verbs

Task

What is happening in the cartoons below? First, work with a partner to describe the action in each sequence. Then, explain how the four sequences fit together to make a story.

   Share your story with other classmates. When you have heard other people's stories, vote on whose story explains the four sequences the best. Whose story makes the most sense and is the most interesting?

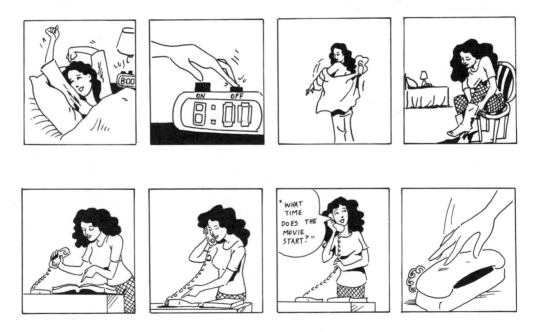

Focus 1

FORM ● MEANING
Phrasal Verbs

FORM
MEANING

- Many common verbs are in two parts: verb + particle. We often call these **phrasal verbs.** It is usually difficult to guess the meaning of phrasal verbs, even if you know the meaning of the parts alone. A good dictionary will help you. For example,

   (a) The waiter did not **wait on** us for a long time. (People who **wait on** tables do very little "waiting"; nor do they do anything "on" tables or "on" people. To **wait on** means to serve people food.)

Exercise 1

Work with your original partner and look back at the cartoons in the Task. For each "frame" (each box) in the sequence, use at least one phrasal verb to describe what is happening, and write it in the list below. Be sure that your description fits in with the story you made up in the Task.

When everyone is finished, share your list with other students. If other students came up with different phrasal verbs to describe the action in the story, add these to your list.

SEQUENCE 1

1. _____

2. _____

3. _____

4. _____

SEQUENCE 2

1. _____

2. _____

3. _____

4. _____

SEQUENCE 3

1. _____

2. _____

3. _____

4. _____

SEQUENCE 4

1. _____

2. _____

3. _____

4. _____

Exercise 2

Add the missing particles to the common phrasal verbs in the following sentences. Use the list below. (Some of these are from your list in Exercise 1.)

break down	call up	find out – discover on team	put off – delay
take back	take up	throw away	get by – accept something
run out have no	look for	call on	throw out even if not
take off have items	put on	wear out	your 1st choice

New Clothes, Old Clothes, Shopping for Clothes

Kent: Why are you taking (1) ___off___ your shoes? I thought you were going to go

for a walk.

Mieko: I am going to put (2) ___on___ my boots. It's raining outside.

Kent: I thought those boots were too small. You said you wanted to take them (3)___back___

to the store. Did you find (4) ___out___ if they have a bigger size?

Mieko: I called (5) _____ up _____ the store. And the salesperson said they ran

(6) _____ out _____ of the old style. But they can look (7) _____ for _____

them in their warehouse if I want to wait. See these boots, though?—I've put

(8) _____ off _____ the decision too long!

Kent: Yes, your boots don't look new anymore. They're beginning to wear (9) _____ out _____

already.

Mieko: Yeah, but fortunately they feel like they're the right size now. They're comfortable.

So I can get (10) _____ by _____ with these, no problem. I hope they last a long

time, like my old ones. I finally threw those old ones (11) _____ away _____ four

years after I bought them!

Exercise 3

Replace the underlined verbs, along with other words in some sentences, with an appropriate phrasal verb from the list below. (Some of these are from your list in Exercise 1.)

pass away   run into   get on
call up   put off   go over
cheer up   drop in on   find out

Keeping in Touch with Friends, Talking about Troubles

1. Sally tried to <u>phone</u> Marie yesterday, but Marie's line was busy. *call up*
2. So she decided to <u>visit</u> her <u>unexpectedly</u>. *drop in on*
3. Earlier that day, Sally <u>saw</u> their friend Ron as he was leaving the apartment building. *ran into*
4. He was ready to <u>enter</u> the bus to go to his sister's house. *get on*
5. He told Sally that his grandfather had <u>died</u>. *passed away*
6. Of course, Sally was sorry to <u>hear</u> that. *find out*
7. She suggested to Marie that the three friends <u>postpone</u> the dinner party they had been planning. *put off*
8. Marie agreed, and she also thought they should do something to <u>make</u> Ron <u>feel better</u>. *cheer up*
9. They decided to <u>go to</u> Ron's sister's, in another part of the city, and give their family a bouquet
   of flowers and a casserole for dinner. *go over*

276

Focus 2

Separable and Inseparable Phrasal Verbs

FORM

- We can separate some phrasal verbs. This means that the particle does not need to directly follow the verb. But if the word that separates the verb from the particle is a **pronoun**, the particle must move to a position after the pronoun.

  - **Separable phrasal verb:** turn on

    (a) She **turned on** the light. OR

    (b) She **turned** the light **on**.

    (c) She **turned** it **on**.
    NOT: She **turned on** it.

  - **Separable phrasal verb:** clean up

    (d) He **cleaned up** his room. OR

    (e) He **cleaned** his room **up**.

    (f) He **cleaned** it **up**.
    NOT: He **cleaned up** it.

- It is difficult to guess whether phrasal verbs are separable or inseparable; this is something that you will need to learn gradually. Even if a pronoun is used with an inseparable phrasal verb, the verb and the particle stay together.

  - **Inseparable phrasal verb:** run into

    (g) Yesterday I **ran into** my friend Sal. OR

    (h) Yesterday I **ran into** her.
    NOT: Yesterday I **ran** my friend Sal **into**.
    NOT: Yesterday I **ran** her **into**.

Exercise 4

Work with a classmate to come up with a list of all the phrasal verbs that you can remember from this unit so far. You have only five minutes to complete this list, so work quickly! If you have extra time, try to think of other phrasal verbs and add these to the list. In order to add these to the list, you must make sure you know the meaning of these phrasal verbs and can use them in a sentence.

When five minutes are up, your teacher will stop you and check to see whose list is the longest. If you added "new" phrasal verbs that aren't in this unit, your teacher will check to see if you can use these correctly in a sentence.

Your next task is to see if you can guess whether the phrasal verbs you have listed are separable or inseparable. Mark these with *S* for *S*eparable or *I* for *I*nseparable. Look back at the way the phrasal verbs are used in sentences to help you decide.

Then check to see how your list compares with the list below.

Separable		Inseparable	
call up	put off	drop in	look for
calm down	take back	find out	pass away
cheer up	take off	get by	pay for
clean up	throw out	get in	run into
find out	turn off	get on	wait on
help out	turn on	get out	
look up	wake up	go over	
pick up	wear out		
put on			

Exercise 5

Are the <u>underlined</u> phrasal verbs correct in the following sentences? If you're not sure, use the list in Exercise 4 and the information in Focus 2. If a phrasal verb is used incorrectly, say what's wrong with it and correct it.

1. Cherie always shows up for work on time. She has to <u>get on</u> the bus at 7:00 A.M., but yesterday she overslept and didn't <u>get it on</u> until 8:00. She was late for work!

2. Last week Sharifah went through her closet and <u>threw</u> all the clothes that were several years old <u>out</u>. Later she <u>found out</u> that her sister had wanted her to keep some of these clothes.

3. When Nina <u>ran Tim into</u>, he pointed out that they had not seen each other for over a year. They promised to <u>drop in</u> on each other more often.

4. After Sandra called, Al gave Graham the message to <u>call Sandra up</u>. Graham tried to <u>call up her</u>, but he couldn't get through because her line was busy.

5. Eli's mother <u>passed last year away</u>. Since she died, he's <u>put</u> the decision about what to do with her house <u>off</u>.

6. When Sally and the other children arrived at camp, the camp counselor went over the rules: The girls had to <u>clean up</u> after breakfast, and the boys had to <u>clean up</u> after lunch.

278

Focus 3

When Not to Separate Phrasal Verbs

USE

- If the noun or noun phrase that separates a phrasal verb is longer than three or four words, it sounds better if the phrasal verb is **not** separated.
  - **Separable phrasal verb:** throw out
    - **(a)** AWKWARD: Last week Sharifah went through her closet and **threw** all the clothes that were several years old **out**.
    - **(b)** CORRECT: Last week Sharifah went through her closet and **threw out** all the clothes that were several years old.
    - **(c)** CORRECT: She **threw** her old clothes **out**.
    - **(d)** CORRECT: She **threw out** her old clothes.

Exercise 6

Sentence 2 in Exercise 5 should not be separated, because the noun phrase is too long (see Example in Focus 3, above). Check the other answers in Exercise 5. Are any noun phrases too long to separate the phrasal verbs? Rewrite the sentence so that it does not sound awkward (if you didn't already do this in Exercise 5).

Activities

Activity 1

Take three separate pieces of paper, and on each one write down a different phrasal verb. Try to choose a phrasal verb that you can "mime"—that is, you can imitate the action—act it out silently—so that others can guess the word(s). For example, *look for* something you lost, *put on* or *take off* clothes, etc.

Your teacher will collect all the phrasal verbs you have written down. Your task is to take three sheets of paper and then mime them in sequence.

Activity 2

See if you can fill in the missing words in the following word puzzle and use each phrasal verb in a sentence. Sometimes the word is a missing particle that all the attached verbs use in phrasal verb combinations; other times the word is a missing verb that all the attached particles use in phrasal verb combinations.

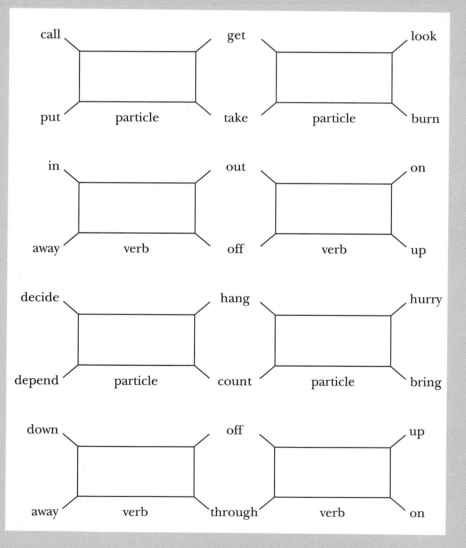

Activity 3

Phrasal verbs are very common in English. The following phrases or sentences are lines from popular songs of the late sixties and seventies. Interview native English speakers (who were born in the late forties through the early sixties) to see if they can recognize these songs. If so, can they remember the lyrics that follow these lines? Who sang the songs?

1. Don't let me down....
2. I'd love to turn you on....
3. Got up, got out of bed, dragged a comb across my head....
4. Each day when I wake up, before I put on my makeup....
5. You just keep me hanging on....
6. Wake up, little Suzie....
7. Hey, you, get off of my cloud....
8. Hang on, Sloopy....

Activity 4

In two teams, you will create a "chain story." You can assign your teacher or one student to write the sentences for the story on the board. The rules are

1. Each team will add only one sentence at a time to the story.
2. Each sentence must make sense as part of the story. In other words, each sentence must be logically "linked" to the previous sentence. (Your teacher will be the judge of this.)
3. Each sentence must contain a phrasal verb, and the phrasal verb must be used correctly.

Every time each team follows these rules correctly, they get one point. The team with the most points wins.

If you want this game to be especially challenging, there is one more rule: The phrasal verb in every new sentence must contain either the same particle as the phrasal verb in the previous sentence, or the same verb as the phrasal verb in the previous sentence.

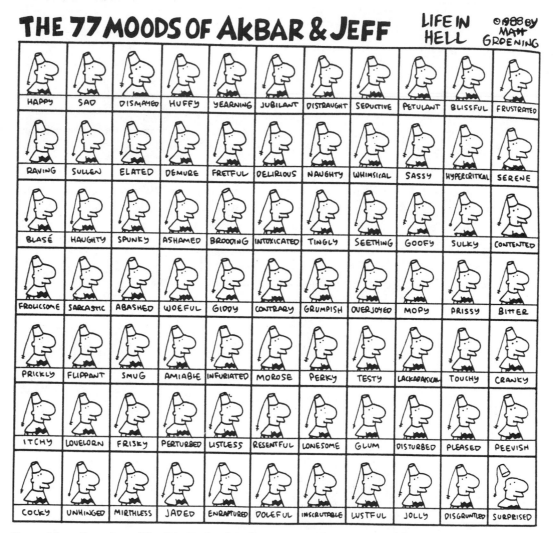

From Matt Groening, *The Big Book of Hell*, Random House, a Division of Pantheon Books, New York (1990).

Task

A. Look through the adjectives above, which describe the many moods of the cartoon characters Akbar and Jeff. You have one minute to find as many *-ing* and *-ed* adjectives as possible, but you can only count the ones for which you know the meaning. Work in pairs or small groups so that you can ask other people about the meanings of words you don't know, or you can divide up the task of looking up the words in a dictionary.

_____-ing   _____-ed

_____   _____

_____   _____

_____   _____

_____   _____

_____   _____

_____   _____

B. Now match the drawings below with these adjectives.

| elated | surprised | contented | seething |
| perturbed | yearning | frustrated | overjoyed |

C. Some of these words are very similar in meaning. Underline those drawings and adjectives under B that show someone feels good. Circle those drawings and adjectives that show someone feels bad.

Focus 1

What -*ing* Words and -*ed* Words Describe

MEANING

- Adjectives that end with -*ing* usually describe the **source**—the thing or person that makes us feel a certain way.
- Adjectives that end with -*ed* usually describe the **emotion**—how we feel about something.

SOURCE/BORING   EMOTION/BORED

Exercise 1

1. Draw arrows that start at the source (the reason for the feeling) and that point to the emotion (the way the person feels).
2. Use the word (on the right) to label the pictures with -*ing* adjectives (which describe the source) and -*ed* adjectives (which describe the emotion). The first one has been done for you.

EXCITED   EXCITING

excite

disgust

284

 shock

 stimulate

 amuse

 embarrass

 surprise

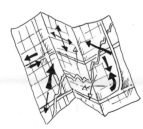 confuse

285

interest

inspire

Exercise 2

Make sentences that describe each of the illustrations in Exercise 1. Use both an *-ing* and an *-ed* adjective.

> **EXAMPLE:** 1. *The TV show was exciting. The person* (or "the TV viewer") *was excited.*

Exercise 3

Choose the correct adjective for each of the following sentences.

1. Melanie likes the family in the apartment above her, but sometimes she feels that their teenage boy is annoying/annoyed, especially when he plays his stereo too loudly.
2. However, she usually finds their presence upstairs very comforting/comforted.
3. Once she heard a frightening/frightened noise outside. She thought it was a prowler, so she called up her neighbors.
4. They invited her to their apartment for a relaxing/relaxed cup of tea and a soothing/soothed conversation.
5. This helped her to calm down, until she was no longer frightening/frightened.
6. Melanie especially likes Jane, the mother. Jane tells Melanie amusing/amused stories about her and her family members' daily life.
7. Jane's husband Bob is a shoe salesperson. Even though this may sound like a boring/bored job, it's not.
8. Lots of surprising/surprised things happen to shoe salespeople. Just last week, for example, a real prince came into the store with his bodyguards and bought 20 pairs of Italian leather shoes.

9. The prince thought Bob was such a polite and amusing/amused young man that he gave him a $50 tip.

10. Of course, Bob thought that this was very exciting/excited, and he took Jane and the family out to dinner that night.

11. Jane works part-time in a pet store as a dog groomer. She says that some of the customers never give their dogs baths. These dogs are sometimes so dirty and uncomfortable that it is shocking/shocked.

12. Jane's stories are so entertaining/entertained that Melanie usually doesn't mind the noise that Jane's teenage son makes.

13. In fact, Melanie was very disappointing/disappointed when she heard that Jane and her family might move.

Exercise 4

Circle all the -ed and -ing words in the following passage. Then decide whether the correct form of the adjective has been used. In other words, are there cases where the -ing adjective is used when the -ed adjective should be used (or vice versa)?

SHELLEY'S ANCESTORS

Shelley had an interested day yesterday. Three of her favorite cousins dropped in for an unexpected visit, and they had a very stimulating conversation. They told each other surprised stories about some of their relatives. Shelley was shocked by some of these stories. For example, when their great aunt—their grandmother's sister—was quite young, she traveled around the world, fell in love with a Dutch sailor, and had a baby but did not get married. Her embarrassing parents disowned her, but many years later they helped her raise the child. Another distant member of the family was a heroin addict in New York in the thirties, and according to Shelley's cousins' mother, he was quite a rude and disgusting fellow. This man's brother was a horse of a different color, though. Apparently he was an inspired and talented poet, who also created amused illustrations for children's books. After hearing all of these stories, Shelley realized that her family history was certainly not bored!

Activities

Activity 1
Can You Top That?

Choose an adjective below that describes an experience you have had (for example, an embarrassing moment, a boring day, an exciting date). Can you think of another experience that is even **more** embarrassing, **more** boring, or **more** exciting than the first one you thought of?

Circulate for 15 minutes and talk to your classmates to see if they have had an experience that "tops" yours—that is, an experience that is even more embarrassing, more boring, or more exciting than yours. After you have spoken to several classmates, report their experience to the class. Take a vote on who has had the most embarrassing, boring, exciting (etc.), experiences.

embarrassing	frightening
boring	horrifying
exciting	entertaining
disappointing	relaxing
shocking	disgusting
surprising	rewarding

Activity 2

Think of someone you know who is quite a character, or in other words, who stands out in some way or is easy to remember because of strong personality characteristics. Describe this person, and be sure to use some *-ed* and *-ing* adjectives in your description.

Activity 3

First think of as many *-ing* adjectives as possible. Your teacher will write each of these on a separate sheet of paper. As the game goes on, your group may add more to the list as needed.

Then you will use these words to play Password in teams or in pairs. In this game, one person (or team), the Clue-Giver, looks at the word on the piece of paper without letting the other person (or the other team) see it. Then they give a one-word clue that describes this word to the other person (or the other team), the Clue-Guesser.

The goal is to have the Clue-Guesser guess the word as soon as possible with as few clues as necessary. But the Clue-Giver can continue to give as many clues as needed in order for the word to be guessed.

Activity 4

Follow the directions for the first part of the activity above, this time using only *-ed* adjectives. Then mime these words, which are written on separate sheets of paper. When you "mime," you "act out" the word or phrase silently by using gestures and facial expressions, or by inventing some silent story that describes the word. The goal of this activity is like the last one: to have the other person (or the other team) guess what the word is as quickly as possible.

UNIT

Conditionals
Future and Hypothetical

Task

What will happen if he doesn't stop drinking, smoking, and gambling? What do you think will happen if he stops drinking, smoking, and gambling?

You are probably sitting in a classroom right now. Or perhaps you are at home or in a library. Probably you are not in either of the following situations:

Which situation would you prefer to be in? Why? What would you do in this situation?

289

Focus 1

Future Conditionals

USE

- We use future conditionals to make predictions about what will happen in the future. **Future conditionals** are formed by:

If Clause + (present tense)	Main Clause *(will/be going to* + **base form of the verb)**
(a) If he doesn't stop drinking	his wife will leave him.
(b) If I study hard,	I'll get a good grade.
(c) If it rains tomorrow,	I'm going to bring my umbrella.

Focus 2

FORM

Word Order in Conditionals

FORM

- In conditionals, the main clause can come first and the *if* clause can come second, with no difference in meaning:
  - **(a)** His wife will leave him if he doesn't stop drinking.
    If he doesn't stop drinking, his wife will leave him.
  - **(b)** I'll get a good grade if I study hard.
    If I study hard, I'll get a good grade.
  - **(c)** I'm going to bring my umbrella if it rains tomorrow.
    If it rains tomorrow, I'm going to bring my umbrella.
- When the main clause comes first, a comma is not needed.

Exercise 1

Make future conditional sentences that are true for you, using the following *if* clauses. If you prefer, you can switch the order of the clauses so that your main clause comes first.

1. If I get an *A* in this class,....
2. If you don't give me ten dollars right now,....
3. If my pants rip,....
4. If I lose this book,....
5. If you shout at me,....
6. If there is a fire alarm,....
7. If I don't see you tomorrow,....

Focus 3

FORM ● USE

Hypothetical Conditionals

FORM
USE

- We can also use conditionals to talk in the present tense about hypothetical situations—situations that will probably not happen. These **imaginary present conditionals**, or hypothetical conditionals, are formed by:

If Clause + (past tense)	Main Clause (*would* + base verb)
(a) If Sherry came to class late,	she would be embarrassed.

(The hypothetical conditional is used in this sentence because Sherry **never** comes to class late.)

- For hypothetical conditionals, when *be* is the main verb in the *if* clause, we use *were,* the **subjunctive** form of the verb *be. Were* is used for all subjects (I, we, you, he, she, it, they).

If Clause + (*were*)	Main Clause (*would* + base verb)
(b) If I were on a desert island,	I would....
(c) If she were a man,	she would....

Exercise 2

The following passage tells a story about Sandira's fantasies. In each sentence, there is a situation that is not real or not likely. In other words, they are sentences that use hypothetical conditionals.

First, tell us what is **not** true about each sentence and the reason it is not true. Then, fill in the blanks in each sentence, and be sure to use the appropriate verb tense.

EXAMPLE: **1.** Sandira _____ go to the movies every week if he _____ (have) enough money.

first step—what is not true about this sentence: Sandira does not go the movies every week because he doesn't have enough money.

second step—fill in the blanks: Sandira _would_ go to the movies every week if he _had_ (have) enough money.

2. If he _____ (be) rich, he _____ never cook at home, and he

_____ always go out to eat.

3. He _____ buy anything he wanted if he _____ (be) rich.

4. If he _____ (have) a girlfriend, he _____ also buy her whatever she

wanted.

5. If he _____ (buy) his girlfriend whatever she wanted, she _____

want to buy more and more.

6. If she _____ (buy) more and more, she _____ eventually run out of

things to buy.

7. She _____ fall out of love with Sandira if she _____ (run out) of

things to buy.

8. If she _____ (fall) out of love with him, he _____ be miserable.

9. If he _____ (be) miserable, he _____ go to the movies every week

to forget about his troubles.

292

Focus 4

Likelihood in Conditionals

MEANING

- The difference between future and hypothetical conditionals is not a difference of time. Both can talk about the future, even though hypothetical conditionals use verbs that look like the past tense form.
- The difference between real and hypothetical conditionals is a difference of likelihood: **future** conditionals talk about what really might happen; **hypothetical** conditionals talk about situations that will probably not happen.
  - **Hypothetical conditional:**
    - **(a)** If Harry became President of the United States, he would. . . . (The hypothetical conditional is used because Harry will probably never become President).
  - **Future conditional:**
    - **(b)** If Al becomes President of the United States, he will. . . . (The future conditional is used because Al might actually become President.)

Exercise 3

Tell whether the situations in the *if* clauses below are future (likely) or hypothetical (unlikely). What do the verb forms tell you about whether or not the situation is likely to happen? Respond to each underlined *if* clause with: "It really might happen" (likely), or "It probably won't happen" (unlikely).

1. <u>If it rains</u>, I will not have to water the garden.
2. <u>If it rained</u>, I would be very happy.
3. Marcy would quit her job <u>if she got pregnant</u>.
4. <u>If I won the lottery</u>, I would travel around the world.
5. Aunt Shira will give us a wedding shower <u>if we decide on a wedding date</u>.
6. <u>If Laurel gets hurt again</u>, her father will make her quit the girl's soccer team.
7. <u>If the baby slept through the night without waking up</u>, his parents would finally get a good night's sleep.
8. Jasmine would buy a big house <u>if she were rich</u>.

Focus 5

FORM ● MEANING

Hypothetical Conditionals in the Past

FORM
MEANING

- Another kind of hypothetical conditional talks about situations in the present or past in which the *if* clause could not be true.

If Clause + (past perfect)	Main Clause *(would/might + have + past participle)*
(a) If he had not robbed a bank, (hypothetical: can't be true because he **did** rob a bank.)	he wouldn't have gone to jail.
(b) If Bill had proposed, (hypothetical: can't be true because Bill did **not** propose.)	she might have married him.

Exercise 4

Complete the following, using the given verb in your answers.

To complete the sentences, think about whether the sentence talks about: a) what really might happen (these sentences use future conditionals); or b) situations in the past in which the *if* clause could not be true (these sentences will use hypothetical conditionals).

EXAMPLE: 1. Gao became a doctor, but if he _____ (be) a truck driver, he _____ (learn) very different skills.

The *if* clause cannot be true, because Gao is not a truck driver; he's a doctor. The hypothetical conditional must be used.

Answer: Gao is a doctor, but if he *had been* (be) a truck driver, he *would have learned* (learn) very different skills.

2. Gao's wife is a doctor, too, but she is thinking of changing careers. If she _____ (change) careers, she _____ (be) _____.

3. Toni has lived in the United States and in New Zealand, so she speaks English, but if she _____ (live) only in Brazil, she _____ (speak) _____.

4. But Toni _____ (speak) _____ if she _____ (move) to France next year.

294

5. Mary's car is old. If it _____ (break down), she _____ (need)

_____.

6. Because Mary has a car, she has driven to school every day this term. But if she

_____ (not + have) car, she _____ (have to) _____.

7. Marcia has applied to graduate school. She _____ (start) school in the fall if she

_____ (get) accepted to graduate school.

8. When Marcia was 21 years old, she quit school for several years to get married and raise

a family. If she _____ (continue) her studies instead of raising a family, she

_____ (begin) graduate school a long time ago.

Exercise 5

Complete the following hypothetical conditionals, using the given verb in your answers.

To complete the sentences, think about whether the sentence talks about: a) a hypothetical situation that will probably **not** happen or b) situations in the present or past in which the *if* clause could not be true.

EXAMPLE: 1. Eloise's husband has always been a thin man in good physical condition. If he suddenly _____ (become) fat, Eloise _____ (be) shocked.
This is a hypothetical situations which will probably **not** happen because Eloise's husband has always been a thin man.
Answer: Eloise's husband has always been a thin man in good physical condition. If he suddenly *became* (become) fat, Eloise *would be* (be) shocked.

2. Eloise started seeing a doctor about her cholesterol problem three years ago. If she

_____ (knew) about her problem earlier, she _____ (change)

her diet years earlier.

3. George's doctor says that one of the reasons George has high blood pressure is that he never

expresses his anger. His doctor says that it is not healthy to "bottle it up." He says that if George

_____ (get) angry once in a while, his blood pressure _____ (not +

be) so high.

4. George never gets angry with his family. His children _____ (run away) from him

if he ever _____ (yell) at them.

5. Dan, who doesn't earn very high wages, has owned Mazda trucks for years. If he
_____ (have) a lot of money to buy a new truck, he _____
(buy) another Mazda.

6. When Dan graduated from college, his father gave him a used Mazda truck. Together they
worked on the truck until it was in excellent condition. If Dan _____ (not +
learn) how to repair Mazdas, he _____ (be) more enthusiastic about other models.

7. People who live in this area have forgotten how to conserve water. If it _____ (not
+ rain) so much last year, people _____ (remember) water conservation practices.

8. People _____ (be able) to water their lawns every day if it _____
(rain) more this summer. However, the forecast is that this area is going to experience a drought
this summer.

Exercise 6

On one sheet of paper, write the following words and complete the hypothetical *if* clause.

If I were _____ . . .

Now, on another sheet of paper complete the main clause.

I would _____ .

a. Your teacher will collect and scramble your *if* clauses and your main clauses, and then you will take one of each. Read your sentence aloud to the rest of the class. Does it make sense?
b. After hearing everyone read their sentences, find the person who has the main clause that matches the *if* clause you have now.
c. Now find the person who has the *if* clause that matches your main clause.

Activities

Activity 1

1. Work in groups of four.
2. First, answer the following questions for yourself. Then do the same thing for each person in your group. Write down what you think each person would be. Don't show the members of your group your paper.
   a. If you were an animal, what would you be?
   b. If you were a color, what would you be?
   c. If you were food, what would you be?

   EXAMPLE: *If I were an animal, I would be a cat. If Terri were an animal, she would be a deer. I also think that Rachel would be a mouse, and Peter would be a flamingo.*

3. When you have all finished, share your ideas and compare what **you** think your group members would be with what **they** think they would be.

	You	Name	Name	Name
(a)				
(b)				
(c)				

Activity 2

In a paragraph or two, describe the most interesting results about **yourself** from the last activity. First tell why you described yourself the way you did. Then tell why you think your group members described you the way they did.

For example, if you said "If I were a color, I would be purple," but everyone else said you would be yellow, give us the possible reasons for these opinions.

Activity 3

Write an imaginary situation or a predicament on a piece of paper. For example, *What would happen if*...everyone in the world were 10 feet taller? *What would you do if*...you found somebody's purse with $200 in it and no identification? *What would happen if*...there were suddenly a huge earthquake?

After you write down one predicament, work with a team to do some "creative brainstorming" to solve the problem or describe the results. Then your team will tell some of your solutions to the other teams. They will try to guess the situation and tell what the *if* clause is. The team that guesses the situation most often wins.

Activity 4

You have all heard of the Beatles. Find people who are familiar with the words to their songs and complete the following lyrics:

(a) If I fell in love with you, would you promise to be true. . . .

(b) What would you do if I sang out of tune, would you. . . .

Peter, Paul, and Mary were a popular folk-singing group in the sixties. Find people who are familiar with Peter, Paul, and Mary lyrics, and see if they can help you finish this sentence:

(c) If I had a hammer . . .

What are the other *if* clauses in this song?

"Carousel" is a famous Rodgers and Hammerstein musical. Find people who can help you complete the *if* clause in the following song:

(d) If I loved you . . .

Question Review

29

From Matt Groening, *The Big Book of Hell*, Random House, a division of Panceon Books, New York (1990).

Task

What questions would you like to ask **your** teacher? Work alone or with other students to fill in the blanks on the following page.

Exercise 1

What are some of the different ways to ask questions? List as many question words or "openers" (*Do...*, *Can...*, *What...*) as you can think of. The Task gives you some ways, but there are more.

Focus 1

Yes/No Questions

FORM
MEANING

- There are several different types of questions. One kind is the **yes/no** question. **Yes/no** questions are called that because they usually require a *yes* or *no* answer, and they are used to seek general agreement/acceptance (yes) or lack of agreement/refusal (no). They usually start with some form of *be* or *do*, or any first auxiliary verb (such as *have*), or with a modal such as *could* or *would*. *Yes/no* questions end with rising intonation.
  - **Examples of *yes/no* questions:**
    - **(a)** Are you going to bed early tonight?
    - **(b)** Did you remember to lock the door?
    - **(c)** Have you been sleeping long?
    - **(d)** Could you close that window, please?
    - Note: This last question requires an action rather than a *yes* or *no* verbal response.

Focus 2

Statement Form Questions

FORM
MEANING

- **Statement form questions** are also a type of *yes/no* question. They appear to be the same as normal statements in form except that they use rising instead of falling intonation. Their function is different, however, because they ask for information that requires a yes or no answer.
  - **Examples of statement form questions:**
    - **(a)** He's a student?
    - **(b)** They've already seen this video?
    - **(c)** You can take the bus to work today?
    - **(d)** She can't find her keys?
- These kinds of questions are fairly common in conversation, but they shouldn't be used too often. They are very informal and sometimes misunderstood because they sound like statements except for the rising intonation.

Focus 3

FORM ● MEANING
Negative *Yes/No* Questions

- We can also state *yes/no* questions in the **negative**. Sometimes if a speaker uses *not* in the question, he or she assumes that the answer is also negative.

  - **Examples of negative *yes/no* questions:**

    (a) Aren't you going to study tonight?
    (Speaker assumes the answer is **no**—The listener is **not** going to study tonight.)

    (b) Won't he teach her how to drive?
    (Speaker assumes the answer is **no**—He **won't** teach her how to drive.)

- Sometimes we use negative questions with *be* and *do* for emphasis, especially with descriptions. These kinds of questions are **exclamatory questions**. With these, the speaker expects agreement instead of a negative answer.

    (c) Wasn't that a lovely play?
    (Speaker expects the listener to **agree**—Yes, it was a lovely play.)

    (d) Doesn't the bride look beautiful?
    (Speaker expects the listener to **agree**—Yes, the bride looks beautiful.)

Exercise 2

Ask another person *yes/no* questions using the following:

1. Can you? . . .
2. Don't you ever? . . .
3. You're going to? . . .
4. Could you? . . .

5. Would you? . . .
6. You know how to? . . .
7. Won't you? . . .

Focus 4

FORM ● MEANING

Wh-questions

- **Wh-questions** are another common kind of question. They are also called Information questions because the answer to the question requires more than just a yes-or-no answer. Most *Wh*-questions begin with words that start with the letters *wh*, and they usually end with falling intonation.
  - **Examples of *Wh*-questions**
    - (a) **Where** is your next class?
    - (b) **Who** would like to borrow my book?
    - (c) **What** happened at the party after I left?
    - (d) **Why** are you smiling?
    - (e) **When** did they eat dinner?
    - (f) **How** old are you?
    - (g) **How many** times have you traveled overseas?
    - (h) **How much** does a new computer cost?

Exercise 3

Fill in the blanks below with an appropriate *Wh*-question word.

1. _____ do you live?

2. _____ is your address?

3. _____ time do you come to school every day?

4. _____ do you get here so early/late?

5. _____ often do you ride the bus every week?

6. _____ way do you come?

7. _____ do you come with?

8. _____ many times have you skipped class this term?

Exercise 4

For each sentence below, ask a question that goes with the answer. When you're finished, compare your questions with other students' questions.

1. **Q:** _____ ?
   A: The closet door is closed because the paint's dry, and so I put everything back in there.

2. **Q:** _____ ?
   A: The broom is in the closet, along with the mop, and some cleaning supplies.

3. **Q:** _____ ?
   A: The vacuum cleaner is probably still in the basement where you left it.

4. **Q:** _____ ?
   A: We need to clean the house because we're having some people over for dinner tonight.

5. **Q:** _____ ?
   A: Martha, Sam, and their kids are coming, and of course our neighbors, the Smiths.

6. **Q:** _____ ?
   A: They met them in the Smith's garden.

7. **Q:** _____ ?
   A: They met them there yesterday morning when we were gone.

8. **Q:** _____ ?
   A: The Smiths were planting flowers.

9. **Q:** _____ ?
   A: Martha and Sam are getting here by car.

10. **Q:** _____ ?
    A: They're taking Sam's car because Martha's is in the shop.

11. **Q:** _____ ?
    A: It's going to cost at least $200.

Focus 5

FORM ● MEANING
Tag Questions

- **Tag questions** are another kind of question that we commonly use in conversation. Like *yes/no* questions, they have to be answered with yes or no. They are used when the speaker predicts either a yes-or-no answer or when the speaker seeks agreement or confirmation.

  - Tag questions start with a statement and end with a "tag,"or shortened question. If the verb in the statement is affirmative (positive), the tag is negative. If the verb in the statement is negative, the tag is affirmative.

  - The speaker expects the answer to agree with the **statement**, not with the tag. If the verb in the statement is affirmative, the speaker expects the answer to be affirmative. If the verb in the statement is negative, the speaker expects the answer to be negative.

    - **(a)** You're going to bed early tonight, aren't you? (The verb in the statement is affirmative, so the speaker expects the answer to probably be yes.)

    - **(b)** You can't go shopping with me today, can you? (The verb in the statement is negative, so the speaker expects the answer to probably be no—I can't go shopping with you today.)

- To agree with a speaker who asks a tag question and to confirm her opinion, use the same as the statement—negative or affirmative, **not** the same as the tag.

  - **Negative statement, affirmative tag**

    - **(c)** Question: You're not cold, are you?
      Answer: No, I'm not. (if you agree with the statement, "You are not cold.")
      NOT: Yes, I'm not.

  - **Affirmative statement, negative tag**

    - **(d)** Question: You're cold, aren't you?
      Answer: Yes, I am. (if you agree with the statement, "You are cold.")
      NOT: No, I am.

FORM ● USE

Tag Question Intonation

- The **intonation** we use in a tag question is very important. If falling intonation is used, the speaker expects the listener to agree with the statement or verify that the statement is true.

   (a) His name is Tom, isn't it?

   (Because falling intonation is used, the speaker expects the listener to agree with the statement–Yes, his name is Tom.)

   (b) It's not going to rain today, is it?

   (Because falling intonation is used along with a negative statement, the speaker expects the listener to agree with the statement–No, it's not going to rain today.)

   (c) His name is Tom, isn't it?

   (d) It's not going to rain today, is it?

   (Because rising intonation is used, the speaker really wants an answer to the question. The speaker doesn't know whether the answer will be yes or no.)

Exercise 5

Your teacher will ask some tag questions. Circle **Y** if you think the expected answer is Yes and **N** if you think the expected answer is No.

1. Y	N	4. Y	N	7. Y	N
2. Y	N	5. Y	N	8. Y	N
3. Y	N	6. Y	N	9. Y	N

Exercise 6

Read each tag question aloud, using the intonation as marked. For each question, tell whether the speaker expects a certain answer or not, and if so, what the speaker expects the answer to be, yes or no. Answer the question the way you think the speaker expects it to be answered.

	(a) Is the speaker sure what the answer will be?	(b) If **yes** to (a), answer the question.
1. It's going to rain today, isn't it?		
2. You don't know where my umbrella is, do you?		
3. You're driving today, aren't you?		
4. It's not my turn to drive, is it?		
5. You made lunch for me, didn't you?		
6. I didn't forget to thank you, did I?		
7. I'm pretty forgetful, aren't I?		

Exercise 7

Look at the picture and then fill in the question or answer in each part below. All questions and answers are about this picture. (Note: For some of these, you will need to guess. There is more than one possible response.)

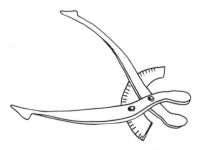

1.   **Q:** _____ ?

    A: Builders, scientists, craftspeople, and others used to use it.

2. **Q:** _____ ?

   A: No, now there are more modern ones.

3. **Q:** When did people use it?

   A: _____ .

4. **Q:** _____ ?

   A: People often used this if they needed it in their jobs.

5. **Q:** _____ ?

   A: You hold it in your hand, and then you pull the legs apart.

6. **Q:** Those aren't real legs on it, are they?

   A: _____ .

7. **Q:** _____ ?

   A: It's made of two kinds of metal.

8. **Q:** _____ ?

   A: Because it's used in heavy and difficult kinds of jobs.

9. **Q:** Who made this thing?

   A: _____ .

10. **Q:** _____ ?

    A: An old farmhouse.

11. **Q:** _____ ?

    A: No, it's old.

12. **Q:** How old is it?

    A: _____ .

13. **Q:** _____ ?

    A: For decoration.

See the answer at the end of this unit.

(Idea from Ilyse Rathet Post)

Activities

Activity 1

Your English teacher has just quit her job and is now sunning on a beach in Tahiti. Your class is desperately searching for a new teacher. You have decided to take matters into your own hands and interview teachers yourselves. One of your classmates is an applicant for the position. Ask him or her some questions about her or his experience, interests, and future goals.

Activity 2

At school, you have recently lost a very unusual and very valuable piece of jewelry, perhaps a ring or necklace. Now you are sitting in class, and you notice that the person sitting beside you is wearing a ring/necklace just like the one you lost. Of course, you would like to ask the person some questions about it to find out if it might be yours.

You might want to role-play this in teams. One team can serve as coaches for the person who has lost the piece of jewelry. The other team can serve as coaches for the person who is wearing the piece of jewelry.

(Idea from Brenda Farmer)

Activity 3

Bring some unusual object to class (or a picture or drawing of the object, as in Exercise 7, above) that your other class members might not recognize, such as a kitchen gadget or an article of traditional clothing. Students can ask the person who brought the gadget any question except "What is it?" and "What is it used for?" The person who guesses correctly is the next one to show his or her object to the rest of the class.

Activity 4

With your classmates, brainstorm a list of questions that are useful for people learning English, in or outside the classroom setting. Vote on the question that is **most** useful and the question that is **least** useful.

To get you started, here are some examples of questions that students have found useful:

What does _____ mean?
Can you repeat that please?

Activity 5

What questions do North Americans ask you the most often? What questions do they **not** ask, which would be common where you come from? Work with your classmates to come up with a list of the most frequently asked questions and the questions that would be asked where you come from but that are not asked in North America.

Activity 6

Bring in a photograph and give it to your instructor. Each student will look at one photograph for 30 seconds and then give it back to the teacher. Other students will then ask the student any questions about the picture they studied and try to guess the situation. Try to use all types of questions: yes/no, Wh-, Statement form, and Tag. The person who brought in the picture can then tell the class whether their guesses were correct or not.

Activity 7

Write a list of questions about a topic that you want to know more about from native English speakers. For example, party behavior/party customs in this country or what are the best topics for "small talk."

Share your list of questions with other students to come up with a questionnaire. Then use this questionnaire to survey native speakers of English. Share the results of your survey with the rest of the class.

Activity 8

What's My Line?

Write down the name of an occupation on a piece of paper and give it to your teacher. Then each of you will take one slip of paper. That is **your** occupation, and you must answer other students' questions about this occupation. Other students will try to guess what your occupation is. They can ask any question except "What do you do?" or "What is your occupation?" Some examples of questions you might ask and be asked are, "Do you work with people?" "Where do you usually work?" "Did you need a college degree to do the work that you do?"

(Idea from Guy Modica)

Answer To Exercise 7:

It's an old-fashioned caliper, used to measure the diameter of tubes, etc.

30

Emphatic Structures

Wh-clefts, Emphatic *Do*,
No versus *Not*

Task

Presidential elections in the United States are held every four years. A friend of yours is involved in a campaign to elect Barbara Tomas as President. She has been asked to make an important speech to persuade people to vote for Barbara Tomas; this speech has to draw attention to the candidate and emphasize her strong points. She has been working on the speech for a while and has nearly finished; however, she can't decide on the most effective way to present some of her ideas. She has written the same thing in several different ways and wants you to help her decide which sounds the most emphatic so that people will remember her message. Look at the notes she has written, and in each group of ideas underline the statement you think will sound best in the speech.

- Support B.T. today!
  ?{ —There's no time to lose.
     —There isn't any time to lose. }?

- We need a new voice in the White House.
  ?{ —B.T. can bring peace, justice and compassion.
     —What B.T. can bring is peace, justice and compassion. }

- Look at what the current president has done.
  ?{ —That isn't the way to run a country. }?
     —That's no way to run a country. }?

- ?{ —Your vote makes a difference.
     —Your vote really does make a difference. }?
     —Your vote really makes a difference. }

° We don't want the same old stuff!

?
{
What we want is a woman in the White House.

We want a woman in the White House.
}

° Other people say they care, but...

?
{
B.T. cares.

B.T. really cares.

B.T. really does care.
}
?

Focus 1

MEANING

Overview of Some Emphatic Structures

MEANING

- There are many ways of emphasizing information in English. The following structures are common:
  - ***Wh*-cleft:**
    (a) Nonemphatic form: The world needs peace and justice. (neutral)
    (b) Emphatic form: *What the world needs* is peace and justice.
    Both (a) and (b) have the same meaning. In (b), the main focus of the sentence is "peace and justice."
  - **Emphatic *do*:**
    (c) Nonemphatic form: I understand. (neutral)
    (d) Emphatic form: I *do* understand.
    (c) and (d) have the same meaning, but (d) places much more emphasis on the statement. Both *Wh*-clefts and emphatic *do* are more common in spoken English than in written English.
  - ***No:***
    (e) Nonemphatic form: She doesn't have any money. (neutral)
    (f) Emphatic form: She has *no* money.
    We often use *no* to make a negative idea more emphatic.

Exercise 1

Turn back to the Task. Check (√) all the emphatic structures you can find. Which statements do you think your friend probably used in her speech? Why do you think this is so?

Focus 2

FORM

Wh-Clefts

FORM

- *Wh*-cleft sentences are divided into two parts:

Assumption (what we already know or understand)		Focus (new information: the emphasized part of the sentence)
(a) What the world needs	is	peace and justice.
(b) What we want	is	a woman in the White House.
(c) Where he goes at night	is	a mystery to me.
(d) What she is	is	an interfering busybody.

The assumption (something we already understand or believe) is introduced by a *Wh*-word and comes at the beginning of the sentence. The focus adds new knowledge or information to the sentence. An appropriate form of the verb *be* links the two parts of the sentence:

(e) What Barbara Tomas brings	is	compassion, peace, and justice for all.
(f) Where he went	was	none of your business.

- When there are two forms of *be* in a sentence, the **second** verb is the verb that links the two parts:

(g) What she is **is** a brilliant politician.

Exercise 2

Match the phrases in Part A with an appropriate word or phrase from Part B. Connect them with an appropriate form of *be* and write the complete sentences in the space below. The first one has been done for you.

A
1. What England is
2. What Florida produces
3. What Alexander Graham Bell invented
4. What Martin Luther King believed in
5. Where the United States President lives
6. What the capital of South Korea is
7. What "mph" means
8. Where the Pyramids are located
9. What Brazilians speak
10. What Americans eat at Thanksgiving
11. What Jimmy Carter was

B
turkey.
Seoul.

Portuguese.
a very small country.
in Egypt.
the 39th U.S. President.
racial equality.
in the White House.
citrus fruit.
the telephone.
miles per hour.

1. *What England is is a very small country.*

2. _____.

3. _____.

4. _____.

5. _____.

6. _____.

7. _____.

8. _____.

9. _____.

10. _____.

11. _____.

Focus 3

How to Use *Wh*-Clefts for Emphasis

USE

- *Wh*-clefts are more common in spoken English than in written English. The *Wh*-phrase refers to a previously expressed (or understood) statement or idea:

  (a) A: How much money does the director earn?

  B: What she earns —⌐ is none of your business!

- We often use *Wh*-clefts to emphasize the difference between two ideas or opinions:

  (b) A: Mozart wrote plays.

  B: No. What Mozart wrote was **music** (not plays).

Exercise 3

Rewrite the underlined words using a *Wh*-cleft. The first one has been done for you.

1. Matt: Henry drives a Porsche.
   David: Don't be ridiculous. <u>He drives a Ford</u>. *What he drives is a Ford.*
   Matt: Really? He told me it was a Porsche.

2. Frank: Margo tells me you're a painter.
   Duane: That's right.
   Frank: Do you sell many of your paintings?
   Duane: Well, actually, <u>I paint houses.</u>

3. Nick: I'm tired. I'm going to take a nap.
   Lisa: No. <u>You need some exercise.</u>

4. Teacher: Do you have any suggestions about how we can improve this class?
   Fusako: <u>We'd like less homework.</u>
   Ricardo: And <u>we'd prefer a test every week.</u>
   Soraya: <u>I need more grammar to pass the TOEFL.</u>
   Bernadine: <u>And I'd like a different textbook.</u> This one is too boring.

5. Oscar: The city council is going to build a new shopping mall.
   Yoichiro: Not another shopping mall! <u>This town needs a good movie theater.</u>
   Oscar: I agree. There's nothing to do here.

6. Howard: Do you know Barry? He writes novels.
   Tessa: No he doesn't. <u>He writes instruction manuals.</u>
   Howard: Well, at least he's a writer.

7. Lee: What are you getting Kim and Hiro for their wedding?

    Stella: They'd really like a microwave, but I can't afford that much, so I'm getting them a toaster.

8. Greg: Mom, can you give me some money? I need a new skateboard.

    Mom: You should get a job. Then you can buy as many skateboards as you like.

    Greg: But all the other kids in my class have new skateboards!

    Mom: I'm sorry, but I'm not giving you any more money.

    Greg: Jimmy's mother always gives him money.

    Mom: Well, I'm not Jimmy's mother.

    Greg: Then maybe I need a new mother!

Focus 4

FORM

Emphatic *Do*

FORM

- We can also add emphasis to a sentence by stressing the auxiliary or the *be* verb:
  - **(a)** I **will** do it.
  - **(b)** He **is** French.
  - **(c)** We **have** finished it.
- In sentences where there is no auxiliary or *be* verb, we can use *do* to add emphasis:
  - **(d)** I like her work.   I **do** like her work.
  - **(e)** They saw us.   They **did** see us.
- We often add extra emphasis with an emphatic adverb like *really* or *certainly*:
  - **(f)** I **really do** like her work.
  - **(g)** They **certainly did** see us.
- In spoken English, emphatic *do* is strongly stressed.

Focus 5

Some Ways to Use Emphatic *Do*

USE

- Emphatic *do* can add emphasis to a whole sentence:

  (a) A: I love you.
  B: Really?
  A: Yes, I really **do** love you.

  This shows how strongly you feel about something or someone. Use it only when you need to add extra emphasis.

- Emphatic *do* can add emphasis to an imperative:

  (b) **Do** come in!

  (c) **Do** give him my best regards!

- Emphatic *do* can contradict a negative statement:

  (d) A: You didn't lock the back door.
  B: You're wrong. I **did** lock it.

  This use of emphatic *do* is very common in arguments. In such situations, the *do* verb generally refers back to a previous statement:

  (e) A: Bob doesn't like this kind of music.
  B: That's not true. He **does** like it.

Exercise 4

Bruce and Gary are brothers, but they often have arguments. Read the following argument and underline all the places where you think it is possible to use emphatic *do*. Rewrite those sentences with an appropriate form of the *do* verb. The first one has been done for you.

Bruce: Did you take my flashlight? I can't find it anywhere.

Gary: Well, I haven't got it. I always return the stuff I borrow.

Bruce: No, you don't.

I do return the things I borrow!
Gary: That's not true! I return the things I borrow! It's probably on your desk. I bet you didn't

look for it there.

317

Bruce: No, I looked on my desk, and it's not there.

Gary: Well, don't blame me. You can't find it because you never clean your room.

Bruce: I clean my room!

Gary: Oh, no you don't!

Bruce: I certainly clean it up! I cleaned it up last night as a matter of fact.

Gary: You didn't.

Bruce: I really cleaned it up last night. Hey, there's my flashlight under your bed.

Gary: Well, I didn't put it there.

Bruce: I bet you put it there. Anyhow, that proves it: You take my stuff and you don't return it.

Gary: I told you before: I return everything I borrow. You just don't look after your things properly.

Bruce: I look after my things. Anyway, from now on, I'm going to lock my door and keep you out.

Gary: You can't. That door doesn't have a key.

Bruce: That's where you're wrong. It has a key and I'm going to lock you out!

Gary: Oh, shut up!

Bruce: Do you know something? You make me sick. You really make me sick.

Gary: Good!

Get together with another student and take the parts of Gary and Bruce. Read the dialogue, paying particular attention to the stress patterns of emphatic *do*. If possible, record yourselves and listen to how emphatic you sound.

Focus 6

Not versus No

- To emphasize a negative statement, we can use *no* + noun in place of *not/n't* + verb:

  (a) They do not have any friends.　　　They have **no** friends.

  (b) Tourists did not come to Birdlip this year.　　　**No** tourists came to Birdlip this year.

- We use *no* with non-count nouns:

  (c) I have **no money**.

  (d) I have **no time**.

  (e) There's **no coffee** in the pot.

- We use *no* with plural count nouns:

  (f) He has **no chairs** in his apartment.

- We use a plural noun here because we are referring to chairs in general, not to one specific chair. Notice the same principle in the following:

  (g) She has **no pets**.

  (h) There are **no teachers** here on Sunday.

- We use *no* with singular count nouns:

  (i) He is taking the bus because he has **no car** today.

  We use a singular noun here because we are referring to a specific car, not to cars in general. We also use a singular noun when we refer to something that is **usually** singular:

  (j) He has **no father** or mother.
  NOT: He has no fathers or mothers.

- *No* is a determiner and we cannot use it with other determiners:

  (k) **No students** came to my office yesterday.
  NOT: No the students came to my office yesterday.

- We can combine *no* with other words to make compounds:

no + one	= **no one**	I saw no one.
no + body	= **nobody**	I saw nobody.
no + thing	= **nothing**	I ate nothing.*
no + where	= **nowhere**	I went nowhere.

  * The first syllable in *nothing* is pronounced differently from the other *no* + compounds.

- In standard English, there is only one negative word in each sentence:

  (l) She **doesn't have any** money. OR She **has no** money.
  NOT: She doesn't have no money.

Exercise 5

Part One. Match the first part of the sentence, (A), with something from (B) that makes sense and is grammatical. The first one has been done for you.

Lily went to a party last night.

A

1. She had hoped to make some new friends, but she didn't meet
2. She had to drive home, so she didn't drink
3. She was very hungry, but when she arrived there wasn't
4. She talked to a few people, but she didn't have
5. Some people were dancing, but Lily didn't have
6. She wanted to sit down, but there weren't
7. Finally, she said to herself: "This party isn't
8. So she went home early and decided not to go to

B

any food left.

anyone to dance with.

any more parties.

anyone interesting.

any fun!"

any alcohol.

anything to say to them.

any chairs.

Part Two. Rewrite each sentence of Part One using *no* or an appropriate *no* + compound. Change the verbs as necessary. The first one has been done for you.

1. *She had hoped to make some new friends, but she met nobody interesting.* _____ .

2. _____ .

3. _____ .

4. _____ .

5. _____ .

6. _____ .

7. _____ .

8. _____ .

Focus 7

When to Use *No*

USE

- Statements using *no* as the negative word instead of *not* emphasize what is missing or lacking. In speaking, we often stress the word *no* for extra emphasis:

  (a) I didn't have any friends when I was a child.

  I had **no** friends when I was a child.

  The *no* sentence emphasizes the lack of friends. The *n't (not)* sentence sounds more like a statement of fact. It sounds less emotional than the sentence with *no*.

- *No* + compound also emphasizes what is missing or lacking:

  (b) I didn't meet anybody interesting at the party.

  I met **nobody** interesting at the party.

  The first sentence sounds neutral, a statement of fact. The second sentence sounds more emotional, emphasizing the lack of interesting people.

  (c) I didn't learn anything new at the conference.

  I learned **nothing** new at the conference.

Exercise 6

Lily is describing the party to her best friend and is telling her what a miserable time she had. Imagine you are Lily and try describing the party from her point of view, emphasizing all the negative aspects of the evening. If possible, record yourself and listen to see how emphatic you sound.

Exercise 7

Emphatic language is very common in political speeches. Read the extracts from speeches below and notice the different ways each speaker uses language to emphasize his message. Underline any examples of the emphatic language discussed in this unit that you can find. Do you notice any other techniques the speakers use to get their points across?

1. Jesse Jackson: Speech to the Democratic National Convention, July 20, 1988

   When I was born late one afternoon, October 8, in Greenville, South Carolina, no writers asked my mother her name. Nobody chose to write down our address. My mama was not supposed to make it. You see, I was born to a teenage mother who was born to a teenage mother. I understand. I know abandonment and people being mean to you, and saying you're nothing and nobody, and can never be anything. I understand. . . . I understand when nobody knows your name. I understand when you have no name . . . I really do understand.

2. Robert F. Kennedy: Speech on the death of Martin Luther King Jr., April 4, 1968

   What we need in the United States is not division; what we need in the United States is not hatred; what we need in the United States is not violence or lawlessness, but love and wisdom, and compassion toward one another, and a feeling of justice toward those who still suffer within our country, whether they be white or they be black.

Activities

Activity 1

Organize a political campaign in class. Divide into groups. Each group represents a new political party. With your group, create a name for your party and draw up a list of all the things you stand for and all the things you will do if you are elected. Make a poster representing your beliefs and prepare a short speech to persuade people to vote for you. Each member of your group should be prepared to speak on a different aspect of your party's policy. Give your speeches to the rest of the class and decide who has the most persuasive approach. If possible, record your speech and afterward, listen to what you said, taking note of any emphatic structures you used and how you said them.

Activity 2

Get together with another student. Think of a relationship or a situation in which people often have disagreements (for example, parent/child; brother/sister; boyfriend/girlfriend; husband/wife; roommate/roommate, and so on). Choose one such relationship and brainstorm all the possible issues these people might argue about. Choose **one** issue and take the role of one of the people in the situation (your partner takes the role of the other). Create the argument these two people might have on this issue. Write your dialogue and prepare to perform it in front of the class. Before you perform, check to see how emphatically you state your point of view. If possible, record your dialogue, and afterward listen to see whether you used any emphatic structures and how you said them.

Activity 3

Get together with another student and look at the poem below.

LESSONS FROM LIFE

I have learned many lessons from life.

I have learned from many different people.

And in many different ways.

What I have learned from my family is _____

What I have learned from my friends _____

What I have learned from _____

And what _____

These are the lessons I have learned

From my life.

Can you think of a way to complete the missing parts? Share your finished poem with the rest of the class.

Activity 4

Get together with another student or form small groups and look at the poem below.

They are old.

They have been here for a long time.

They are _____ .

They have no _____ and no _____ .

Nobody _____ .

What they really want is _____ .

They are old.

They have been here for a long time.

Brainstorm all the things that *they* could refer to in this poem. Choose **one** and complete the poem with this as your topic. Give the poem a title. Display your poem so everyone can enjoy it.

Activity 5

Look at the poems you and your classmates wrote in Activity 4. Decide which ones are pessimistic and which ones are optimistic about the topic. Choose one of the poems (it can be the one you wrote or it can be one written by other students). Using this poem, try to rewrite it from another point of view. For example, if the original poem was pessimistic, can you rewrite it so that it is optimistic? If it was optimistic, can you rewrite it so that it is pessimistic? Share your results with the rest of the class.

Appendix

Irregular Verbs

Simple Form	Past (-ed)	Past Participle	Simple Form	Past (-ed)	Past Participle
be	was, were	been	let	let	let
become	became	become	lie	lay	lain
begin	began	begun	light	lit, lighted	lit, lighted
bite	bit	bitten	lose	lost	lost
bleed	bled	bled	make	made	made
blow	blew	blown	meet	met	met
break	broke	broken	pay	paid	paid
bring	brought	brought	put	put	put
build	built	built	quit	quit	quit
buy	bought	bought	read	read	read
catch	caught	caught	ride	rode	ridden
choose	chose	chosen	ring	rang	rung
come	came	come	rise	rose	risen
cost	cost	cost	run	ran	run
cut	cut	cut	say	said	said
do	did	done	see	saw	seen
draw	drew	drawn	sell	sold	sold
drink	drank	drunk	send	send	sent
drive	drove	driven	shine	shone	shone
eat	ate	eaten	show	showed	shown, showed
fall	fell	fallen	shut	shut	shut
feed	fed	fed	sing	sang	sung
feel	felt	felt	sit	sat	sat
fight	fought	fought	sleep	slept	slept
find	found	found	speak	spoke	spoken
fly	flew	flown	spend	spend	spent
forget	forgot	forgotten	stand	stood	stood
freeze	froze	frozen	steal	stole	stolen
get	got	got, gotten	swear	swore	sworn
give	gave	given	swim	swam	swum
go	went	gone	take	took	taken
grow	grew	grown	teach	taught	taught
have	had	had	tear	tore	torn
hear	heard	heard	tell	told	told
hide	hid	hidden	think	thought	thought
hit	hit	hit	throw	threw	thrown
hold	held	held	understand	understood	understood
hurt	hurt	hurt	upset	upset	upset
keep	kept	kept	wake	woke	woken, waked
know	knew	known	wear	worn	worn
lay	laid	laid	win	won	won
lead	led	led	write	wrote	written
leave	left	left			

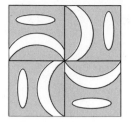

Index